THROUGH THE FIRE

THROUGH THE FIRE

JOSEPH M. STOWELL

While this book is designed for the reader's personal enjoyment and profit, it is also intended for group study. A Leader's Guide with Victor Multiuse Transparency Masters is available from your local bookstore or from the publisher.

VICTOR

BOOKS a division of SP Publications, Inc.
WHEATON. ILLINOIS 60187

Offices also in
Whitby, Ontario, Canada
Amersham-on-the-Hill, Bucks, England

Unless otherwise noted, Scripture quotations are taken from the *Holy Bible: New International Version,* © 1973, 1978, 1984 by the International Bible Society. Used by permission of Zondervan Bible Publishers. Other quotations are from the *King James Version* (KJV).

Recommended Dewey Decimal Classification: 248.4
Suggested Subject Heading: FAITH

Library of Congress Catalog Card Number: 85-50320
ISBN: 0-89693-601-5

C O N T E N T S

IN ANTICIPATION

Difficulty is part of the fabric of our existence. As Job states, "Man is born to trouble as surely as sparks fly upward" (Job 5:7).

Our trouble is based in the reality that we are a fallen race; we live in a fallen place. When we understand the depth of that reality, we should no longer be surprised at pain. If anything, we should be surprised that there is pleasure. Life's great challenge is how to deal successfully with pain. This book is about the challenge of pain.

For me, life has had its good times and its bad times, its problems and its pleasures. I have lost and I have gained. I have stood by, walked with, wept with, and rejoiced with many who have suffered far more deeply than I have.

In it all, I have discovered something very special. A light in the darkness. I have discovered that with God, there is significance in pain. That trouble can be a prelude to triumph. That difficulty need not damage us but that it can, to the contrary, be a source of growth. I have discovered that pain by the wonderful power of God can be productive. That it is a process with a purpose. That it indeed works "together for good to them that love God, to them who are the called according to His purpose" (Rom. 8:28, KJV).

I wish to share that discovery with you. Specifically. In terms of real people who live today and real people who live in the pages of Scripture. People just like you and me.

In this book you will discover three realities about pain—the process of pain, the seven purposes of pain, and how to persevere in pain.

For those who hurt, it is my prayer that these truths will become your strength and comfort.

For those whose lives may be momentarily free from pain, I trust that these pages will provide a clear understanding of pain that will prepare you to survive successfully when trouble becomes your portion.

IN APPRECIATION

As I have been writing this book, I have become aware of my deep indebtedness to:

The many who have graciously consented to let us look into the darkest moments of their lives that others may see the light.

The delightful flock of God at the Highland Park Baptist Church who received these messages with an open heart to the voice of God.

The staff of men with whom I serve. Their effective sharing of ministry enables me to study and write.

The professional advice of my editor, Becky Dodson, who refines my work with a gracious spirit and an insightful hand.

The capable counsel and conscientious assistance of my secretary, Monalee Ferrero.

The encouragement, wise input, and patience of my wife, Martie. Without her, I would not be writing this book.

The reality that in God "we are hard pressed on every side, but not crushed; perplexed, but not in despair; persecuted, but not abandoned; struck down, but not destroyed" (2 Cor. 4:8-9).

The love of Christ in which we can confidently ask, "Who shall separate us from the love of Christ? Shall trouble or hardship or persecution or famine or nakedness or danger or sword? No, in all these things we are more than conquerors through Him who loved us. For I am convinced that neither death nor life, neither angels nor demons, neither the present nor the future, nor any powers, neither height nor depth, nor anything else in all creation, will be able to separate us from the love of God that is in Christ Jesus our Lord" (Rom. 8:35, 37-39).

This book is lovingly dedicated to my wife's
parents,
JOHN AND JANE BENNETT,
who through difficult
times have faithfully reflected the
grace and glory of
God

PART ONE

THE PROCESSES OF PAIN

PAIN
The Source and Solution of Pain

The transatlantic connection was weak and interrupted, yet the reality of a broken heart on the other end was clear. It was Martie, Craig's wife. As she spoke, everything inside me wanted to scream.

Craig and I had grown up together. His parents sponsored our church youth group and many said Craig and I looked like brothers. After attending the same college in the Midwest, I went off to seminary. Craig married Martie, a pretty coed in his class, then enlisted in the Air Force.

We lost touch. Our paths merged again a few years later as I assumed my first pastorate. It soon became apparent that our lifestyles had taken two divergent tracks. Craig had lost interest in the Lord and lived in the fast lane. Yet, in time, God began to work in Craig's and Martie's hearts. They recommitted their lives to Him and became active in our small fellowship of believers. Craig taught our high school boys and Martie taught the girls. Craig and Martie became the first missionaries to go out from that blossoming work and we all felt a tremendous sense of fulfillment and joy as they headed for Haiti.

They had been in Haiti only a week. Martie brokenly told me that Craig had been diving and after his last dive had floated to the surface, back up. He was taken in a jeep across the rugged trail to a primitive hospital, where he now lay with a broken neck. His head and face were swollen beyond recognition. Craig didn't make it through the night. Martie was there alone—a widow.

To me, it made no sense. My pain was filled with questions that seemingly had no answers. Inside, I felt a heavy sense of despondency and defeat. I kept asking God why. *Why now? Why them? Why this pain?* Somehow way down inside, Craig's death clashed with my belief that God was a wise, all-powerful, and loving God.

PAIN—A COMMON EXPERIENCE

Though all of us may not experience trouble of this magnitude, not one of us is exempt from the problem of pain. From disease to disablement to despair, depression, death, divorce, discouragement, disappointment, and a host of other problems, difficulty is an unwelcome reality of life. There are no guarantees. Even for the most comfortable of us, trouble may be waiting in the wings of the next moment of our lives. Don't let trouble surprise you. "Man is born to trouble as surely as sparks fly upward" (Job 5:7). Life *is* difficult. The sooner we realize and accept that reality, the more prepared we will be to deal with the problem of pain.

What do we do when we're troubled by trouble? How do we handle the dismantling of our faith by pain? How do we stand when life falls in around us? What is left when our lives seem dark, wasted, and worthless?

Many of us find that pain conflicts with our biblical view of a good and powerful God and therefore we find it too risky, too unsettling to deal with pain head on. Unfortunately, we retreat to pious sounding statements and hide under hollow phrases that have little meaning and no healing value.

Should we bother to take the risk to understand pain? Absolutely! God has given us answers to the problem of pain. Knowing about pain from the vantage point of God's truth equips us to make it through with our hands held high in victory. Seeing trouble through God's insightful eyes will not only help us, but it will also equip us to comfort others as we walk with them through their deep waters.

SETTING ASIDE THE MYTHS

Knowing the truth about the source and solution of pain requires that we first set aside the myths. Responding to difficulty from the perspective of these false assumptions will only compound our pain. It is imperative that we remove these barnacles from our minds if we intend to sail through troubled waters with power.

Pain is punishment. When impacted by difficulty, our first response often is to reflect on "why we're being punished." We reach back in the past to find some failure that will explain our pain. This compounds our pain with guilt. While it is true that God *does* discipline us with difficulty, it is also true that *not all* difficulty is discipline.

The disciples wrongly assumed that pain was punishment when they asked Christ, "Who sinned, this man or his parents, that he was born blind?" (John 9:2) Christ responded, "Neither this man nor his parents sinned, but this happened so that the work of God might be displayed in his life" (v. 3).

Pain is nonproductive. In this pleasure-mad world, trouble is seen as an unproductive experience. We fail to realize that pleasure often corrupts us, while pain is an able instrument that brings us to a clear sense of ourselves and our true values. When tragedy strikes, all that is fleeting and temporary, all we had wrongly valued so highly, is quickly relegated to its rightful position. Trouble brings God, family, friends, and our inner selves into sharp focus.

Romans 5:3-5 affirms that trauma *can* be productive:

> We also rejoice in our sufferings, because we know that suffering produces perseverance; perseverance, character; and character, hope. And hope does not disappoint us, because God has poured out His love into our hearts by the Holy Spirit, whom He has given us.

Pain is indicative of spiritual failure. Some of us falsely equate the "good life" with God's blessing. We are told that if we have plenty of faith, we can be happy, healthy, and wealthy. Trouble then becomes a reflection of a less than productive faith and, thus, a bad reflection on our spiritual standing and ability. But if trouble is a sign of a faithless and immature life, why did some of God's best people suffer ill health, trouble, and trauma of all kinds? (See 2 Cor. 12:7-10; Phil.

2:25-27; 1 Tim. 5:23; Heb. 11; 1 Peter 2:21-24.) Spiritual giants are *not* exempt.

Pain is bad. Paul writes, "And we know that in all things God works for the good of those who love Him, who have been called according to His purpose" (Rom. 8:28). This statement clearly affirms that pain can be categorized as *good*. How quick we are to define *good* only in terms of comfort, convenience, and prosperity—when often pain is the means to something good. This does not discount the trauma of pain and suffering. It does, however, enable us to see pain in the "big picture" as part of a process that ultimately is good.

Pain is incompatible with a God who is good and all-powerful. In his best-seller, *When Bad Things Happen to Good People,* Harold Kushner writes: "The misfortunes of good people are not only a problem to the people who suffer and to their families. They are a problem to everyone who wants to believe in a just and fair and livable world. They inevitably raise questions about the goodness, the kindness, even the existence of God" (Schocken, pp. 6-7).

Though difficult, this question is not unanswerable. As we shall see, God's claims to be good and all-powerful are not in contradiction. In fact, His goodness and power offer the solution to our pain.

Dismissing these myths liberates us to see the truth clearly. Knowing the truth about pain is the first step to a productive and victorious response to life's difficulties.

THE SOURCE OF PAIN

Originally God created an environment that was painless and trouble-free. All of creation was a revelation of God's glory.

From the stars in the heavens to man himself, the primary purpose of creation was to demonstrate God's glory (Gen. 1:26-27; Ps. 19:1).

At the center of this demonstration of God's glory was the element of choice. Man would *choose* to obey and worship God (Gen. 2:15-17). This would dramatize that God is worthy of man's loyal allegiance. If God had not given man the option to choose, man's spontaneous love for God would have meant nothing.

Yet, in that important element of choice was the potential for failure. The potential to sin. And that's exactly what happened (Gen. 3:1-6). God is no more responsible for our failure than a teacher who gives a test in which there is the potential for a student to fail. *We* made the choice to sin, not God.

When the choice was made to sin, Adam and Eve transferred their loyalty to Satan and Satan established himself as the god of this world (2 Cor. 4:4). Since Adam and Eve were the governors of all creation (Gen. 1:26), Satan was able to intrude into creation and gain control by controlling them. As Paul states so clearly, all of us and all of creation now groan under the curse of sin (Rom. 8:18-23). Sin is the source of pain and Satan is the source of sin.

There was no sorrow until sin and Satan stepped onto the landscape. As soon as sin hit the scene, as God had warned, it brought death. Death with all of its trouble and pain. There was the loss of self-esteem (Gen. 3:7), a sense of personal shame and alienation (v. 8), the reality of fear (v. 10), the transference of guilt to another (v. 12), pain in childbirth (v. 16), and exhaustion in labor (vv. 17-19). By the time Genesis 4 is concluded, Adam and Eve have experienced the trauma of jealousy, anger, murder, the pain of the loss of a child, the agony of the consequence of sin, and an increase in violence in a godless culture.

God's Word consistently defines the source of pain in terms of Satan and sin. All of Job's suffering was at the hand of Satan (Job 1—2). Paul's thorn in the flesh was a messenger of Satan (2 Cor. 12:7). The weaknesses of our bodies are a result of the curse of sin (Rom. 8:23). Pain is a part of God's judgment on sin (Gen. 3).

Why does Satan want to bring trouble and pain into this world? Satan's intention is to defame the glory of God. *All* of creation was created to glorify God. God intended that we would join the created world in reflecting the beauty and strength of His magnificent character. Pain and trouble are the graffiti that Satan scrawls across the face of God's glory. It's his way of getting to God, of staining God's reputation.

A beautiful office building was being built near our home. I watched it take shape and come to completion. It was the the glory of the architect, a great reflection on the builder. It was beautiful. It enhanced the landscape and all that was around it. One morning as I drove by I was surprised by an ugly scene. In the night, vandals had sprayed the exterior walls and windows with black paint. The beauty was gone; the glory was marred.

That's Satan's purpose in pain.

Think of how successful Satan has been. When was the last time you heard Satan and sin blamed for war, blight, starvation, and crime? Who gets blamed for murder, rape, greed, trauma, trouble, and difficulty? Most people blame God.

It is clear that Satan does not care about us or our environment. He only seeks to use us and abuse us to deface God's glory. Satan once desired God's glory for himself and was denied (Isa. 14:12-17). He now hates God and seeks to destroy His reputation through sorrow and pain.

TWO REALITIES

In light of the source of pain, there are two realities that must be understood.

First, we live in a fallen system; therefore, *no one is exempt.* Jesus wept (John 11:35). Timothy needed some wine for his stomach's sake (1 Tim. 5:23). Epaphroditus was sick unto death (Phil. 2:27). Paul lived with his thorn in the flesh (1 Cor. 12:7-10). Trophimus was left at Miletos, sick (2 Tim. 4:20). The apostles were martyred. First-century Christians were burned at the stake and some were fed to lions. In this sin-bound system, trouble is certain. No one is exempt, not even the best of us.

On hot summer days I used to go swimming in a lake where we vacationed. The water felt good and I always enjoyed the swim. In that lake were small leeches that would attach themselves to my legs and feet. I hated them. They were gross, unpleasant, and repulsive to me. But, if I was going to swim, the leeches would be there. They went with the territory. Trouble is like that. It goes with the territory of life.

Paul recognized this reality when he wrote that our bodies are not yet redeemed. They are still bound by the problem of sin.

We know that the whole creation has been gro
ing as in the pains of childbirth right up to the
present time. Not only so, but we ourselves, who
have the firstfruits of the Spirit, groan inwardly as
we wait eagerly for our adoption as sons, the
redemption of our bodies (Rom. 8:22-23).

From colds to cancer to crabgrass to cruelty. No one is
exempt. Don't let trouble surprise you:

Second, since we live in a fallen system, our *righteousness
may be the cause of pain and trouble.* Christ warned His disciples, "I have told you these things, so that in Me you may
have peace. In this world you will have trouble. But take
heart! I have overcome the world" (John 16:33). We are
instructed that righteousness will create friction in an unrighteous world (John 15:18-25; Phil. 1:29; 3:10; 1 Peter 2:19-
24). Paul wrote, "In fact, everyone who wants to live a
godly life in Christ Jesus will be persecuted" (2 Tim. 3:12).

It was the experience of Christ, Moses, Joseph, Job, the
prophets, the five slaughtered missionaries to the Auca Indians, and others like Chester Bitterman who were martyred
for their work in world missions. Pain and trouble come
from taking a stand for righteousness.

When our astronauts come back into the earth's atmosphere, their ship must be protected by technologically ad-
vanced heat shields. The space capsule creates tremendous
friction by moving into the atmosphere with great velocity.
The atmosphere resists the reentry. As we move through
this alien, anti-God atmosphere, the friction at times may
create some heat. No righteous person is exempt. Yet he
who sows in tears shall reap in joy (Ps. 126:5; John 16:20).

SOLUTION TO PAIN

If God is good and all-powerful, then why doesn't He do something about our pain?

He has.

Note that on the heels of the warning of impending trouble, Christ affirms, "In the world ye shall have tribulation; but be of good cheer; I have overcome the world" (John 16:33, KJV). God's work of overcoming the problem of pain is actualized in three dimensions.

In the *past*, Christ overcame the world through the cross and His resurrection. Satan, sin, and death were defeated. The victory was sure, accomplished on our own turf and in our own history (John 12:31; 16:11; 1 Cor. 15:55-57; 2 Cor. 5:17).

This finished work guarantees the *future* dimension of Christ's overcoming power. God will judge Satan and all those not redeemed from the curse of sin. Hell will be their eternal portion (Rev. 20:10-15). The sin-cursed heaven and earth will be destroyed (Rev. 21:1; 2 Peter 3:7, 10, 12). God will create a totally new, sin-free creation to His glory where we the redeemed will live forever, locked into His righteousness through the work of Christ. There will be no more sorrow, for

> He will wipe every tear from their eyes. There will be no more death or mourning or crying or pain, for the old order of things has passed away. He who was seated on the throne said, "I am making everything new!"
>
> Then He said, "Write this down, for these words are trustworthy and true" (Rev. 21:4-5).

Pain is not permanent for those in Christ Jesus. As Paul said, "I consider that our present sufferings are not worth comparing with the glory that will be revealed in us" (Rom. 8:18).

Christ is the solution to the problem of pain by His past victory at the cross and His future work of putting pain permanently away. I can almost hear someone saying, "There you go again, talking about the past and the future with no relevance to today." I'm reminded of the Queen in Lewis Carroll's *Through the Looking Glass* who complained, "Jam tomorrow and jam yesterday—but never jam today."

But there *is* jam today. There is an overcoming work of Christ in the *present.* For reasons known best to God, we live in a time when Satan has been permitted to function though he has already been judged. In the face of Satan's work the present overcoming work of Christ provides two dynamics that give us the ability to conquer.

First, God's grace. Paul realized that God's grace was sufficient for His trial (2 Cor. 12:7-10). God's grace is God's help, His enablement. Isaiah spoke of it graphically:

But now, this is what the Lord says—He who created you, O Jacob, He who formed you, O Israel: "Fear not, for I have redeemed you; I have called you by name; you are Mine. When you pass through the waters, I will be with you; and when you pass through the rivers, they will not sweep over you. When you walk through the fire, you will not be burned; the flames will not set you ablaze" (Isa. 43:1-2).

I have stood by as many suffered deep pain. Through their tears, they testify to an inner strength. I walk away and say to myself, *I don't know how they do it*. Then I am reminded of the reality of God's grace. Grace comes with pain. It is God's gift sent with the messenger of Satan. God's grace is our overcoming strength.

The second dynamic is God's glory that can be revealed even in the darkest seasons of life. This was true of the man born blind (John 9:1-3). Fanny Crosby, blinded early in life by a careless physician, glorified God by translating her spiritual sight into song; she wrote hymns that have taught and blessed millions. Joni Eareckson's witness for Christ is magnified from a wheelchair. Christ delights in turning the tables on Satan's best efforts to defame Christ's name. He glorifies His name even through pain and trouble. This is the overcoming work of Christ today.

Their baby had died in its crib. Revived by the emergency squad, he lived with mechanical support for three days. Through their tears and confusion, the parents portrayed a unique strength. Christian friends were faithful and loving in their support. The hospital personnel began by observing, "You must be religious." As the hours passed, the medical staff recognized something deeper than religion. Before the ordeal was over, they had asked about the faith that strengthened this couple in the midst of their pain.

In the face of death, Christ offers grace and glory. The grace and glory of God don't make trouble any less painful, but they do fill pain with strength and purpose. Grace and glory are the present victory that overcomes the world. In Christ, temporary loss is always in the context of ultimate gain. Overcomers reach for the grace and go for the glory.

A few months after Craig's death, Martie wrote:

> Thank You, Lord, for choosing me
>   to view Your pain at Calvary.
> Your tearstained paths of grief You share
>   With me these days because You care.
> Thank You for the time I cried
>   within the garden, by Your side,
> "If it be possible for Thee,
>   please, God, this cup remove from Me."
> Thank You, too, for the burden I bear
>   for the loneliness, and for the despair,
> For beneath this cross, and on this road
>   I feel, in part, Your heavy load.
> Thank You for the desperate plea,
>   "God, why hast Thou forsaken Me?"
> "Because," You answer tenderly,
>   "I have a special plan for thee."
> Thank You for the hope You've given,
>   for the truth that You have risen.
> I, too, from suffering shall rise
>   as I fulfill Your plan so wise.
> Thank You, Lord, for letting me say,
>   "By grace I've suffered in Your way."
> And, may I nevermore depart
>   from this, the center of Your heart.
>   MARTHA BALDOCK FELLURE

2

CERTAINTIES
Clinging to the Exclamation Points

Pain will make or break us. There really is no middle ground. Sadly, the landscape of life is littered with the pieces of fragile lives shattered by the blows of pain.

But periodically there are those who stand among the broken pieces. They have taken the painful blows and transformed them into grace and glory. They are not made of stronger stuff, but they have an orientation in pain that preserves them in the midst of trouble. They have a working knowledge of the rules of the game.

Getting through life victoriously demands a willingness to know and play by the rules. It would be insufficient to expect you to succeed at basketball by simply showing you a ball and a court. It would even be insufficient to tell you that the object of the game was to place the ball through your hoop more often than your opponent. If you entered the game with only that knowledge, you would soon be a frustrated participant. The first time someone stole the ball from you or blocked your shot, you'd shout "UNFAIR!"— yet, in reality, that's a part of the game. You would feel cheated simply because you didn't fully understand the rules.

You'd be left with a choice. You could pout in the middle of the court; you could shout caustic remarks at the referee as you bitterly stomp off the floor; you could even tell everyone how much you hate basketball. Or you could regroup, learn more about the game, get back in, and participate successfully.

Living is much like that. If we falsely suppose that life consists of being born, being saved, being comfortable, dying, and going to heaven, then we have totally misunderstood life and we will probably be consumed by it. Existence here on earth is a highly competitive experience. And while none of us asked to be put in the game, we find ourselves in the midst of its fast-paced, confusing, and often painful scramble. We either play it by adjusting to the fundamental rules or we fight against it. No one has ever won by bucking the rules.

John Wooden, the successful former basketball coach of the UCLA Bruins, once stated that the key to the great strength of his teams was their mastery of the fundamentals. If pain is to make us and not break us, then we too must master the fundamentals. Two fundamentals are foundational to our successful response to trouble. When we respond to pain in the context of these two truths, we successfully survive. The pain becomes a productive agent of change. What is more important is that when we cling to these certainties in the process of our pain, we reflect God's grace and glory to a watching world.

THE DIVINE SENTINEL

The first certainty in pain is that *EVERYTHING that comes into our lives comes through the sovereign permission of God.*

The World Series finally came to Detroit in 1984. The tickets were sold out the first few days of their availability and many who wanted to go could not. At game time security guards were posted at the gates of Tiger Stadium. The only ones permitted in were those who had tickets. All others were excluded.

God stands like that at the gate of our existence. Nothing—absolutely *nothing*—passes into our lives that has not first passed by the sovereign authority of God. He is the divine sentinel. This truth is nowhere better illustrated than in Job.

When Satan came to God in Job 1, he claimed that Job loved God only because God had abundantly blessed him. Satan asked, "Hast not Thou made an hedge about him, and about his house, and about all that he hath on every side?" (Job 1:10, KJV) God obviously had not planted shrubs around Job's home. Satan was simply saying that God had not permitted any pain or trouble to come Job's way. Satan used this slander to malign the worthiness of God to receive man's unqualified allegiance, so God granted *permission* for Satan to test the depth of Job's allegiance. He permitted Satan to withdraw all the blessings of home and health and at the same time refused to permit Satan to take Job's life (vv. 11-12). God stood as the sentinel at the gate of Job's existence.

Not only does the picture of Job illustrate God's work in permitting or excluding pain, but God's very nature as the sovereign, all-knowing, all-powerful God guarantees this foundational principle. God is sovereignly and ultimately in control of all the universe (Job 38—41). His sovereignty guarantees His oversight of all the affairs of man (Isa. 37:16; Num. 23:19). His omniscience assures us that He is totally aware of all that transpires (Ps. 139:1-6). His power guarantees that He is able to withhold or permit all that seeks to intrude into our lives (2 Cor. 13:4; Phil. 3:21).

While it is true that all pain comes through the sovereign permission of God, its *source* may vary. If we envision our lives like a one-room house with an entrance in each wall, we would note that pain enters from different sources. Some pain is caused *directly* by Satan. Job's experience is the classic example.

On the other hand, pain may come to us because of the disobedience or carelessness of others. The agony of Joseph's separation from his family was a direct result of the willful sin of his brothers.

There are times when pain enters the door of our own disobedience or carelessness (1 Peter 2:19-20). Jonah purposely disobeyed and the trauma of a three-day blackout in an underwater hotel became his portion.

At times our trauma is permitted by God as a direct result of our obedience. The disciples obediently took the boat across the lake and even though they obeyed, they experienced a storm which threatened their lives. That storm was used by God to teach them firsthand a lesson in faith (Mark 4:35-41).

Many times pain is a combination of two or three of these sources, as it was in the crucifixion, where God's Word states of Christ, "This man was handed over to you by *God's* set purpose and foreknowledge; and you, with the help of

wicked men put Him to death by nailing Him to the cross"
(Acts 2:23).

The principle of God's permission is a tremendous source
of personal encouragement and security in the midst of pain.
The psalmist writes: "The angel of the Lord encamps around
those who fear Him, and He delivers them" (Ps. 34:7). It
would be a frightening reality if our trials could escape the
notice and permission of our God. How dreadfully helpless
and vulnerable we would be.

One evening after soccer practice I was walking home
from high school when three men jumped my friend and me
and began beating us for no apparent reason. I vividly
remember seeing a man walking toward us; I thought that he
would surely come to our defense. As we called for help, he
calmly walked by, ignoring our pleas for aid. Our only
glimmer of hope was gone! We were completely vulnerable.
No believer ever needs to feel the helpless agony of sensing
that God is unaware. There is security in knowing that
nothing circumvents God's throne. He is aware of and atten-
tive to our plight.

The old Swedish hymn by Lina Sandell Berg says it best:

> More secure is no one ever
> Than the loved ones of the Saviour—
> Not yon star on high abiding
> Nor the bird in homenest hiding.
>
> God His own doth tend and nourish,
> In His holy courts they flourish;
> Like a father kind He spares them,
> In His loving arms He bears them.

Neither life nor death can ever
From the Lord His children sever,
For His love and deep compassion
Comforts them in tribulation.

Little flock, to joy then yield thee!
Jacob's God will ever shield thee;
Rest secure with this Defender—
At His will all foes surrender.

What He takes or what He gives us
Shows the Father's love so precious;
We may trust His purpose wholly—
'Tis His children's welfare solely.

Understanding that all my pain is by God's permission is important. Yet in and of itself, that knowledge is not enough. Without the second certainty, we may be tempted to think that God is cruel, unfair, and insensitive in permitting pain into our lives.

THE GUARANTEE OF HIS NATURE

The second certainty in pain is that *ALL that God permits is guaranteed by His nature*. God cannot be unfaithful to Himself!

Skeptics delight to ask, "Can God make a rock so big that He cannot move it?" No matter how you answer the calculated riddle, you limit God. If He cannot move the rocks that He makes, then He is not all-powerful. If He can't create rocks that big, then again He is limited. The right answer to the question is that God cannot do anything contrary to

Himself. He is limited by His own nature. God cannot be all things to all people. He can only be those things that are consistent with Himself. He is truth; therefore, He cannot lie (2 Sam. 7:28). He is eternal; therefore, He cannot cease (Deut. 33:27). As Paul states, "He cannot disown Himself" (2 Tim. 2:13).

While we choose to love or to be merciful, God is quite different. God doesn't choose to love or to be merciful. God *is* loving. He *is* merciful. All of His attributes are intrinsic to His being.

Each morning I get up, shave, shower, and dress. I go to the office, study, interact with the staff and leaders of the church, go to lunch, then return to the office. About 2 P.M. I consider lying down for 15 minutes, but my phone buzzes and there is another call to take, another sermon to prepare, another article to write.

Our dog Paddington is quite different. She gets up when she wants to, eats when she wants to, goes outdoors when she wants to, comes in when she wants to, and when she wants to sleep, she drops on the spot and sleeps as long as she wishes.

There are times I wish I were a dog. But, like it or not, I can't be. My humanity is *intrinsic* to me. I didn't choose to be human. I *am* human. My nature dictates all that I am and all that I do.

God's nature is intrinsic. It guarantees all that He does. He cannot deny Himself. This truth has tremendous relevance to the problem of pain and the certainty of His permission. Since God cannot violate His nature, all that He permits must be consistent with what He is. This guarantees that God is never destructive, malicious, or wrong in what He permits. It means that we can see our pain within the context of God's nature.

God's goodness (Ps. 34:8; Rom. 8:28). It is difficult to see the goodness of God in the context of our pain. Yet the psalmist writes, "Taste and see that the Lord is good" (Ps. 34:8). Often we equate goodness with painlessness, yet that is an insufficient equation. Is surgery good? Is birth good? Even the truth occasionally hurts. There are many occasions when we readily recognize that the process of pain is good. We must be sure to distinguish between goodness and comfortableness. Comfort is not always good and goodness is not always comfortable. God never promised us a life of "birth to death" comfort. God may not always be comfortable, but He is always good; all that He permits can come to ultimate good for both our own sakes and His glory (Rom. 8:28-39).

God's creative power (Gen. 50:20; Rom. 5:3-5; James 1:2-5). Constantly demonstrated through biblical history is God's power to take the most negative situations and turn them into positive realities worthy of His praise. Nothing transcends the power of God. Whether our difficulty is from Satan, others, self-inflicted, or experienced in the process of our obedience, it is God's prerogative to rearrange, reconstruct, reinterpret, and realign the situation to bring glory and praise to His name. Joseph, when faced by his brothers in Egypt, proclaimed, "You intended to harm me, but God intended it for good to accomplish what is now being done, the saving of many lives" (Gen. 50:20). Even Christ's tragic death on the cross was transformed by the power of God into great and positive results.

God's justice (Ps. 37:28). In all that God permits, justice must prevail. We often feel that God has cheated us or treated us unfairly because we have been granted pain. But "the Lord loves the just and will not forsake His faithful ones. They will be protected forever" (Ps. 37:28).

Though God is always just, life and others around us are often unfair and unjust. Yet, God's justice guarantees that all that is unfair will ultimately be dealt with. We are naive to assume that all of life in its fallen condition will be fair and just. It is only safe to realize that God is just and that in His time and way He will deal with injustice. Paul writes that God "will pay back trouble to those who trouble you and give relief to you who are troubled" (2 Thes. 1:6-7).

God's holiness (Ps. 145:17). God is perfect and never makes a mistake. His perfection grows out of His holiness. The holiness of God is a foundational attribute of God's nature. It is also a foundational support in the process of pain. Our holy God is governed by impeccable, flawless behavior. He indeed is "holy in all His works" (Ps. 145:17, KJV).

God's total knowledge (1 Cor. 10:13; 2 Peter 2:9). The reality that God knows all about us is significant in the face of pain. "No temptation has seized you except what is common to man. And God is faithful; He will not let you be tempted beyond what you can bear. But when you are tempted, He will also provide a way out so that you can stand up under it" (1 Cor. 10:13). Since God knows our load limit, when necessary, He will limit the load. That assures us that though we may bend, we will not break.

God's total knowledge also lifts our sense of despair. In difficulty, we often sense that there is no way out. That's when deep despair corners us. Trouble can be like a room with no doors and no windows, a room with walls that are

closing in. I love the verse that says, "The Lord knows how
to rescue godly men from trials" (2 Peter 2:9). When there
seems to be no options of release, God already knows how
to deliver you. He has options you've never dreamed of!
God's accurate timing (Ps. 31:14-15). God is always on
time—never too early, never too late. Shadrach, Meshach,
and Abednego probably wondered about God's sense of
timing as the guards pushed them into the fire. But it was *in*
the fire that God met them and gave them a testimony to
turn a pagan king's heart to the true and living God (Dan.
3:4-30). "I trust in you, O Lord; I say, 'You are my God.'
My times are in Your hands" (Ps. 31:14-15).
God's consistent presence (Heb. 13:5-6). God's promise that
He will never leave us nor forsake us is a certainty that brings
great assurance and security in trouble. We must remember
what God said through the Prophet Isaiah:

> O Israel, fear not; for I have redeemed thee, I have
> called thee by thy name; thou art Mine. When
> thou passest through the waters, I will be with
> thee; and through the rivers, they shall not over-
> flow thee; when thou walkest through the fire,
> thou shalt not be burned; neither shall the flame
> kindle upon thee. For I am the Lord thy God, the
> Holy One of Israel, thy Saviour (Isa. 43:1-3, KJV).

God assured Joshua, "Have I not commanded you? Be
strong and courageous. Do not be terrified; do not be discouraged, for the Lord your God will be with you wherever
you go" (Josh. 1:9). David knew that even in the face of
death, a sense of God's presence took away the fear (Ps

23:4). Therefore, we can "say with confidence, 'The Lord is my helper; I will not be afraid. What can man do to me?' " (Heb. 13:6).

God's certain purpose (Rom. 8:28-29). God never wastes our sorrows. In Him, there is certain purpose in pain. There are the purposes of conformity to His image, usability in His service, purity in our lives, a new sense of God-sufficiency, effectiveness in ministry, and identity with Christ.

Our God of purpose grants pain only with a productive end in mind. That's why it is said of Christ that He willingly endured the cross for "the joy set before Him" (Heb. 12:2).

God's unfailing love (Rom. 8:35-39). Paul asks:

> Who shall separate us from the love of Christ? Shall trouble or hardship or persecution or famine or nakedness or danger or sword? . . . No, in all these things we are more than conquerors through Him who loved us. For I am convinced that neither death nor life, neither angels nor demons, neither the present nor the future, nor any powers, neither height nor depth, nor anything else in all creation, will be able to separate us from the love of God that is in Christ Jesus our Lord (Rom. 8:35, 37-39).

God loves us and actively involves Himself in meeting our needs. No trouble can separate us from Him.

God's productive empathy (Heb. 4:15-16). "But you don't understand what I'm going through," she said. "No one understands."

She was right. I didn't understand. I'd never been there

before. I could help her, but I couldn't feel with her. He-brews 4:15 guarantees that God is a God of empathy: "We do not have a High Priest who is unable to sympathize with our weaknesses, but we have One who has been tempted in every way, just as we are—yet with out sin." Christ has experienced it all—rejection, loneliness, disappointment, physical pain. In this great heart sensitivity, He activates His mercy and sends "grace to help" in our time of need (v. 16).

CLING TO THE CERTAINTIES

In trouble, we find refuge and repose in these certainties that are guaranteed by God's very nature. This is exactly what God's Word means when it exhorts us to be strong *in the Lord* and the power of His might (Eph. 6:10). If you have ever walked through a swamp you know that your feet are constantly searching for something solid to stand on—a rock, or perhaps a stump. When you find something solid, you immediately stand on it. Though you're still in the swamp, you are safe and secure. God's nature is our rock.

We can choose either to sink in the mire of all that is uncertain or to climb onto the rock of what is certain and view our troubles from God's vantage point. Is it any wonder that Scripture constantly demands that we trust in God? If we trust in anything else or anyone else, we will surely fold. Our only hope is in God.

My children dislike getting shots. As our name is called in the doctor's waiting room, I pick up my daughter and move toward the room where the shot will take its toll. As we near the room, she realizes what is ahead. The closer we get, the tighter her little arms close around my neck. As we open the door and see the nurse in her white uniform pushing the last bubble of air out of the needle, Elisabeth clings to me tenaciously. The closer she gets to pain, the more tightly she clings to her father.

During Job's tragic suffering, his wife said, "Curse God and die!" (Job 2:9) Job affirmed, "Though He slay me yet will I trust in Him" (13:15, KJV). Since God could not deny His nature, Job would not deny his God. Job knew that pain was only possible through the permission of a holy, good, powerful, and fair God.

Where is God when it hurts? Right there at the gate of your existence guaranteeing all that comes by His certain nature.

> Hast thou not known? Hast thou not heard, that the everlasting God, the Lord, the Creator of the ends of the earth, fainteth not, neither is weary? There is no searching of His understanding. He giveth power to the faint; and to them that have no might He increaseth strength. Even the youths shall faint and be weary, and the young men shall utterly fall; but *they that wait upon the Lord* shall renew their strength; they shall mount up with wings as eagles; they shall run, and not be weary; and they shall walk, and not faint (Isa. 40:28-31, KJV).

PROCESS
Do All Things Really Work Together for Good?

Surgery. Many of us have experienced it. It is inconvenient, painful, unpleasant, frightening, and disruptive. Yet surgery is good. We choose to submit to it. Why? Because the pain is worth the gain. Because there is a purpose for the pain.

Purpose always restructures perspective. As a boy, I disliked getting out of bed for school. I can remember begging my dad for 5 extra minutes. But on the days we were going fishing, I anxiously awoke at 5 in the morning, ready to go. Somehow *that* was different.

God's Word assures us that, for the believer, *all* pain is a process with a purpose. In fact, God guarantees the purpose to be good:

> And we know that in all things God works for the good of those who love Him, who have been called according to His purpose. For those God

foreknew He also predestined to be conformed to the likeness of His Son, that He might be the firstborn among many brothers (Rom. 8:28-29).

BALANCING THE GUARANTEE

Two issues must be dealt with in the face of this familiar passage. First, God does not intend for us to become spiritual masochists. I suspect that some Christians feel that progress comes only in pain and that there is something inherently wrong with pleasure and success. Though growth and progress may be more difficult in pleasure, God affirms that *all* things work together for good (Rom. 8:28).

Pleasure, success, and good things are as significant as suffering. We must learn with Paul the "secret of being content in any and every situation, whether well-fed or hungry, whether living in plenty or in want. I can do everything through Him who gives me strength" (Phil. 4:12-13). Let us never forget that God "richly provides us with everything for our enjoyment" (1 Tim. 6:17). Our assurance is that whether in pleasure or in pain, God is able to bring about that which is good.

Second, we are prone to become shallow and flippant with a guarantee like this. In the midst of heavy hurt, it's easy for us to nestle up to a friend and say, "Well, brother, remember Romans 8:28." I stopped my casual use of this verbal panacea for all our ills the day I received this letter.

Dear Pastor Stowell:
I've thought of communicating with you on your current sermon theme [Romans 8:28]. Since

August 30, 1979, every time that theme ⌐
I am painfully reminded of my brother's death by
suicide.

He left a widow with two small daughters. I had
to identify him for the coroner and tell my parents
what had happened. Then I had to clean the walls
and ceiling and furniture of his blood and flesh, as
he had shot himself in the head. The legacy of his
death confronts us on a regular basis.

I have asked myself often—*what good was there in
his death—to us—or to him?* There is no answer.

Except for a handful of close personal friends,
the local church was not much comfort. Most
acted as though it never happened.

How do you make Romans 8:28-29 make sense to a
hurting friend like this? It *does* make sense. And as it does, it
becomes a tremendous source of strength. The guarantee of
Romans 8:28-29 contains three truths that fortify us in
difficulty.

GO WITH WHAT YOU KNOW

Trouble brings with it a whole bucketful of emotions. Despair, hurt, revenge, self-pity, anger, sorrow, and a dozen
other feelings. If we are not careful, these feelings will
dominate and disorient us from what we know. Emotions
redirect our thoughts and detour our commitments. We tend
to distort what we know by how we feel.

*Our resource in pain is not what we feel, but rather what we
know.* Romans 8:28 literally says that we have an absolute

knowledge. Our knowledge in pain is not a *hope so* or maybe or *might be*—but a *know so* reality. While our emotions are like quicksand, absolute knowledge is a bedrock.

Notice that each major section on difficulty in Scripture begins with an appeal to what we know. "We also rejoice in our sufferings, because *we know* that suffering produces perseverance; perseverance, character; and character, hope" (Rom. 5:3-4). Likewise, James 1:2-4 directs us to "consider it pure joy, my brothers, whenever you face trials of many kinds, because *you know* that the testing of your faith develops perseverance. Perseverance must finish its work so that you may be mature and complete, not lacking anything." When our emotions jade our perspectives, God's truth doesn't change. Truth is truth regardless of how we feel.

More than one pilot has lost his life in a plane crash because he let his feelings determine his direction. When out of sight of land, lost in the clouds or in the darkness, a pilot will often become disoriented. He can be flying in a tight circle and feel like he is flying straight ahead. He has to rely not on how he feels, but on his instruments. They represent the truth and even though it goes against every grain of his intuition, he must let the instruments guide him.

God's truth gives us a unique edge to which we can cling in trouble. This catalog of truth is in contrast to the pagan mindset which clings to axioms such as:

- Grin and bear it.
- Don't get mad, get even.
- Look for the silver lining.
- Pull yourself up by the bootstraps.
- Think positively.

Unfortunately, you can't always grin as you bear it and getting even makes for more trouble. Bootstraps have a way of breaking and the silver lining is often little more than tinfoil.

Sometimes in pain we discount the value of truth by saying, "But I only know God's truth from the neck up; it doesn't make sense in my heart." That's OK! It's what you know from the neck up that will enable you to keep your head up. In time, it *will* make sense in your heart. Just don't let go of the truth.

What do we know? We have learned that with God there is the victorious, overcoming work of grace and glory through difficulty, that in trouble there are certainties to which we can cling. The certainty of His goodness, creative power, justice, holiness, and total knowledge. We know that He is a God of accurate timing, consistent presence, certain purpose, unfailing love, and productive empathy. We know that He must always relate to us in the context of these truths.

We know that trouble develops character (Rom. 5:3-5) and that trials equip us to be more useful (James 1:2-5). Because of Romans 8:28, we know that *good* is the ultimate purpose of the process of pain. Knowing and clinging to what we know makes the difference. Truth is our stability factor in trouble.

I'll never forget the 1980 winter Olympics when the American hockey team defeated the Russian team on its way to the gold medal. Coming home after church that Sunday morning, I turned on the television and to my surprise the U.S. team was winning the game! I sat glued to my set, agonizing with every play of the puck and every shot at the goal. It was moment-to-moment trauma. My competitive juices had me in a knot. And then the buzzer sounded . . . we had won!

That evening we watched a replay of the entire game. Same plays with the puck, same shots on goal, but a completely different attitude in my heart. I sat back with popcorn and Pepsi, put my feet up, and watched the game with joy. What made the difference? Knowledge!

A friend was telling me about devastating months of depression that she had gone through. Nothing had seemed to help. The only thing that kept her from breaking was "the truth that heaven is real." That bit of basic knowledge kept her head above the swirling flood of her emotions.

Another friend, whose child had died two months before, told me, "It hurts more now than it did then. All we have is the fact that God is sovereign and omniscient," he said as his voice broke. That's pretty basic, but it was enough to get him through.

As God's people we have the advantage of truth in pain. It's a definite edge in trouble. It's our resource. Cling to it.

PAIN IS A PROCESS

We specifically learn in Romans 8:28 that pain is a process. Foundational to the acceptance of pain is the awareness that God has us in process. None of us is what God wants us to be. Though God loves and accepts us the way we are, He sees all that we can become. Pleasure has a way of making us very satisfied with ourselves. Pain catches our attention so that God can process us into His dream for our lives.

This work of God is defined in several dimensions. First,

it is *all-encompassing*. Since God works in *all* things, we are guaranteed that whatever He permits—whether pain or pleasure, bane or blessing—He is able to use it to process us.

Beautiful automobiles are especially alluring. They become useful and beautiful through a process. The process involves a design concept that is reached through bending, banging, shaping, heating, riveting, fusing, and tightening. It is a slow process as the assembly line moves at an almost imperceptible speed, but it is a certain process with a desirable goal. Hundreds of component parts make up the whole. Some are unsightly and added under great pressure, while others beautify; yet each is essential to the process.

The truth that pain is a part of God's process is seen in the context (Rom. 8:18, 23, 26). To wish to be processed by God and yet resist the presence of pain is to be a hunk of shapeless steel that wishes to be a Mercedes-Benz without the process.

Not only is God's process all-encompassing, but we also *know* from Romans 8:28 that it is a *continuous* process. "God works" is a present, continuous tense verb. God will never abandon His purpose for us or the process to accomplish it.

I don't know about you, but I have a lot of unfinished projects in my basement. Things I tore apart to restore. Antiques that I have begun to refinish. God has no abandoned projects.

The third dimension to this all-encompassing, continuous process is the most significant of all. It is the reality that this is a *divinely supervised* process. Note that Romans 8:28 says "*God* works." Behind the scenes of my life story is the hand of God. Moving, changing, limiting, applying pressure, providing strength, rearranging. God is the one working all things to good.

Auguste Bartholdi went from France to Egypt in 1856. He was awestruck by the grandeur of the pyramids, the magnitude of the mighty Nile, and the beauty of the stately Sphinx of the desert. His artistic mind was stimulated. While on this trip he met another visitor to Egypt, Ferdinand de Lesseps. Ferdinand was there to sell an idea. An idea to cut a canal from the Red Sea to the Mediterranean Sea that would save merchant ships the long journey around the tip of the African continent. Auguste was taken by the concept. He decided to design a lighthouse to stand at the entrance to this canal.

It wouldn't be an ordinary lighthouse. It would symbolize the light of the Western civilization flowing to the East. It took 10 years to build the Suez Canal. For 10 years, Auguste worked on his idea. He drew plans, made clay models. He scrapped plan after plan. Then he had the right one. It was the perfect design.

Only one problem remained. Who would pay for it? He looked everywhere, but no one was interested. The Suez Canal was opened—without a lighthouse. Auguste went back to France defeated. Ten years of toil and effort wasted.

You would have liked his idea. It was a colossal robed lady that stood taller than the Sphinx in the desert. She held the books of justice in one hand and a torch lifted high in the other to light the entrance to the canal.

After Auguste returned to France, the French government sought his artistic services. His planning and designing culminated in the Statue of Liberty lighting the New York harbor. His disappointment had turned to delight.

If in the normal course of life things that seem to be

disappointing, difficult, and defeating can be processed into that which is magnificent and significant, how much surer is this process with the hand of our wise and powerful God guaranteeing the outcome.

We must take caution, however, against slipping into an irresponsible fatalism that sees God as both the source and the processor of pain. Within the "all things" of Romans 8:28 are choices and consequences that are a part of being fallen people who live in a fallen place.

Edith Schaeffer in her book, *Affliction,* tells of a child who fell off a cliff to his death and of another who slipped through the ice into a frozen lake. Did God push the child from the cliff? Did God push the boy through the ice? No, these tragedies occurred because we live in a fallen place and are a part of a fallen race. It was a choice to venture too close to the edge of the cliff. A choice not to check the safety of the ice. But it is the powerful, creative hand of God that takes these tragic settings of life and works them all to good.

Life is a lot like a jigsaw puzzle. Often our lives can seem like a thousand pieces spilled onto the table of our world. Confused, disoriented, senseless, and tragic, but then God comes and carefully, wisely, in His way and in His time, puts the pieces together. In the end, the puzzle spells *good.* That's what we know. As Paul affirms, "He who began a *good* work in you will carry it on to completion until the day of Christ Jesus" (Phil. 1:6).

PAIN—A PROCESS WITH A PURPOSE

The third dynamic is that God has no process without purpose. The guarantee of Romans 8:28 states that we know that God processes in us all things toward good. That's His purpose. For the believer, there is no pain without purpose of a good result.

I stood in the church foyer and said to a set of relieved parents, "God has certainly been good to spare you your son." The night before, their son had been in a terrible auto accident. He was rushed to a hospital over an hour away for special treatment. All night he hung onto life by a thread. He had made it! Standing next to his parents was another couple whose daughter had been killed in a car wreck a few years before. It was then that it hit me. *Had God not been good to them? What was I saying about my definition of good? What must my comment have meant to the parents who were less fortunate?*

God defines *good* for us in Romans 8:29. The text says that this process is for those who have been called according to God's purpose. What is God's purpose? According to verse 29 it is to conform us to the image of His Son and that is *good*. Anything that will bring us to reflect the glory of Christ in and through our lives is good. Whatever it takes, pain or pleasure, is good if it conforms us to His likeness. That's God's goal in the process of pain. He takes all that He permits and makes it a part of the process to bring us to reflect the image of Christ.

Our family was at a conference some time ago and Matthew, our youngest child, fell and broke his wrist. I have never seen anything like it. His arm took a sharp left at his wrist and then turned again to resume its normal journey to his hand. It was grotesque.

We rushed Matthew to the hospital where the doctor began to set his wrist. I watched as the doctor pulled and twisted Matthew's arm. The doctor began to perspire and I felt like jumping up and pulling the doctor off my son. But I simply sat and watched. I knew that Matt's arm needed to be restored to its original design and purpose. But pain and several weeks of inconvenience would be a part of the process.

We too, broken and hurt by sin and self-will, must often be reset by a good and loving God. Set back into the image of His Son. Set back into compassion, righteousness, and love. Set into the original purpose of His glory through us. Good things may have to come in painful packages.

God not only has the intention of processing us to what is good, but He also has the power to complete the project. I love what the Prophet Isaiah said when he wrote that God would "comfort all who mourn; to appoint unto them that mourn in Zion, to give unto them beauty for ashes, the oil of joy for mourning, the garment of praise for the spirit of heaviness; that they might be called trees of righteousness, the planting of the Lord, that He might be glorified" (Isa. 61:2-3, KJV).

Michelangelo sculptured "David" out of a hunk of stone. Other artists take colored oils and canvass and create masterpieces. Beams of steel are bent and welded to create monuments to who knows what in our city squares. But I have never seen an artist even attempt to make something beautiful from ashes. Only God can do that (Isa. 61:3).

God is able to bring the love of Christ into our lives. It may take some brokenness. It may require that we go through a time of need to become sensitized to the needs of others. If it requires pain to do that, then it is good.

Can you weep with those who weep? God may need to stain your cheeks with tears so that you can genuinely empathize as Christ does.

Are you self-sufficient? The tragedy of our affluent culture is that we rarely sense we *need* God, when in reality we desperately do. God may need to strip away some of your security, as painful as that may be, to conform you to the God-sufficiency that Christ displayed; that would be good.

Are you faithless? It may take the impact of a tragedy for you to experience the reality of God that you may learn to lean on and trust Him like Christ did; that would be good.

Are you proud, indifferent, carnal, selfish, unforgiving, negative, or angry? God has something better. The lifestyle of His Son.

God is able to transform us. He knows what is best. He knows what it takes. He will, as the loving, all-powerful sculptor, chip away until Jesus is seen in the hardened hunk of our lives.

For those of us who know God, pain is a process with a certain purpose. We don't make it through tough times. We are made through tough times—made into the beauty of Christ Jesus. And in that perspective, the pain is worth the gain.

PART TWO

THE PURPOSES OF PAIN

POWER
The Trouble with Righteousness

Ron had an outstanding position with a major cable television network. He was rising in the company and had been assigned to manage the operation in our area. As he grew in Christ, it became increasingly clear that the TV programming offered on his network was a contradiction to his commitment to Christ.

Crossroads . . . the place where pivotal choices are made.

For Ron, the most comfortable choice was to keep his job and compromise his commitment to righteousness. The other option would prove to be painful, difficult, and uncertain. Ron knew what was right. He made his choice and walked right into difficulty. Resigning his post with nowhere to go meant moving his family, beginning the difficult task of reestablishing himself in the business community, and living on a dwindling income to say nothing of the end of a blossoming and fulfilling career.

Righteous choices often bring trouble. Good people do suffer; bad people do prosper. It's an issue with dynamics rooted in an understanding of where we live and who we are. But righteous choices bring a unique power through the pain.

WHERE WE LIVE

We live in Satan's domain. We move through a network of values, thoughts, actions, and perspectives that are hostile to righteousness and truth. God's Word calls this system the world (John 15:18-25; 16:33). Anything alien or threatening to the world system is resisted and reproved by the world.

As we pioneer into organ transplants, medical technology struggles with the problem of rejection. Our bodies are designed by God to resist any alien object. Immediately upon intrusion, blood cells rush to the sight to shield against contamination. Our body mechanism chokes off any blood supply to the foreign object. It is isolated and barricaded so that it is unable to influence or threaten the system.

The world system responds the same way to righteousness. Therefore, as we choose righteousness, that choice may very well spell trouble. Through history it has meant rejection, poverty, misfortune, and death. In our own generation, believers in Africa have died gruesome deaths for their unflinching choice to be righteous. In one country, the government demanded that the people return to their animism and spirit worship. Pastors and deacons who refused were buried alive up to their necks in the city square. Stakes were then driven through their heads. The scene remained for days for all to take notice, including the wives and children of those who suffered for righteousness.

WHO WE ARE

We live in an alien system that is hostile to us because we are the children of God. As children of God, we choose righteousness and in so doing become instant sources of irritation to an unrighteous world.

There is no illustration more profound than the dynamics around Christ's life. His righteous *words* and His righteous *actions* were such strong sources of conviction that they ultimately led to His crucifixion. He recognized this when He told His disciples, "If I had not come and spoken to them, they would not be guilty of sin. Now, however, they have no excuse for their sin. He who hates Me hates My Father as well. If I had not done among them what no one else did, they would not be guilty of sin. But now they have seen these miracles, and yet they have hated both Me and My Father" (John 15:22-24). He went on to tell the disciples that as they reflected Him, they too would feel the pressure (vv. 18-25). The fact is that the work of the Spirit through us will be a work of conviction, reproof, and judgment. Jesus said, "[The Holy Spirit] . . . will convict the world . . . concerning sin, because they do not believe in Me; and concerning righteousness, because I go to the Father . . . and concerning judgment, because the ruler of this world has been judged" (16:8-11, NASB).

For us, a choice for righteousness may very well be a choice for difficulty. Both history and the Word of God clearly depict what we can expect from righteousness in an unrighteous environment.

RELIGIOUS INTIMIDATION

Choosing to worship in a manner consistent with biblical truth will be a source of conflict in the world's system of religion. Paul states that part of Satan's system is a false, humanized system of religion. Satan sends his angels as "ministers of righteousness" (2 Cor. 11:13-15, KJV).

The roots of religious intimidation go back to Cain and Abel. Abel worshiped in a way pleasing to God. Cain too was religious; he brought an offering. But he wanted religion on his own terms. Refusing to repent and worship in a way pleasing to God, Cain had to deal with Abel, the source of his conviction. Abel's continued presence and continued worship was a reminder to Cain of his own religious rebellion. Finally, Cain killed Abel to eliminate the pressure (Gen. 4:1-8).

Christ brought religion on God's terms and the self-styled religionists of His day, the Pharisees and Sadducees, ultimately killed Him. True religion is intolerable in a false religious system.

Mankind has an insatiable appetite for religion, but we fashion God according to ourselves. We recreate and distort Him into the form of our own tastes. In the process, His justice, righteousness, wrath, and holiness are lost. He becomes less than sovereign. His Word is not authoritative, but rather an assemblage of interesting tales to be applied in a convenient, nonthreatening way. In this form, God and His Word do not impede our personal tastes and our desired behavior. As Paul says, "People will be lovers of themselves, lovers of money, boastful, proud, abusive, disobedient to their parents, ungrateful, unholy . . . having a form of godliness but denying its power" (2 Tim. 3:2, 5).

As a result, themes such as God's wrath, His justice, His judgment, and His salvation become less than acceptable in a humanized religious system. Those who proclaim these truths are branded as extremists, bigots, manipulators of fear, fundamentalists, overemotional, unintellectual, selfish, and old-fashioned. Though no one dies in America today for righteous worship, the reputation, prestige, and prominence of the righteous in the secularized religious community is maligned and true worshipers are often held in low esteem.

Recently a couple who had been attending a church whose ministry reflected the secular system received Christ. In their newfound faith they discerned the nonbiblical, humanistic stance of their church. They began fellowshipping with us. The wife of this couple and a friend went back to the rector of their former church to discuss the difference. When she discussed the Bible, the rector told her she was *foolish* to take it literally. When she discussed salvation, he said she was *selfish* to be so concerned about her own condition. After all, Christ's death had saved everybody. When she talked about how much she appreciated hearing the Word taught, he accused her of *idolatry*. Worshiping the pastor and worshiping the Bible.

The religious system of this world seeks to belittle and intimidate us. We must expect it and be ready to bear the reproach of truth, refusing to do anything less than worship the Lord (John 4:24).

SOCIAL REJECTION

It was a large family, twelve children to be exact. All boys. They were, as the Bible says, evil. Except for one. He had chosen righteousness instead of acceptance by his brothers and he paid for it. For being so good, God permitted him to be sold as a slave to a remote country. He was not easily discouraged. In the absence of every positive influence in his life and in the midst of devastating loss, he affirmed his righteousness afresh. Having risen to a place of influence in his master's home, his boss' wife tried repeatedly to seduce him. She finally grabbed him and he fled. She was incensed and framed him. He landed in jail. Three years in the slammer for doing what was right.

Why?

Joseph was an intolerable source of conviction to the world around him. His righteousness revealed the unrighteousness of others. That is why the Word of God warns us that the godly shall suffer persecution and encourages us to bear up under the pain of unjust suffering. If we suffer because of our conscience toward God, our endurance is commendable before God (1 Peter 2:19-20).

One of the hardest demands of discipleship is to endure the pressure that comes from affirming righteousness in the face of unrighteousness. It's hard for a pastor who wants to be well-liked to proclaim righteousness. Tough for a businessman to refuse to go along with a partner in a shady deal. Though there are many times when a choice for righteousness may mean exclusion from a group, loss of a friendship, or being totally misunderstood, righteousness must prevail. It is the cause of Christ in us.

Social repercussions mustn't surprise us. Christ told the disciples that the Holy Spirit would "convict the world of guilt in regard to sin and righteousness and judgment" (John 16:8). The Spirit's work in us may well create pain.

LOSS OF PRESTIGE, PLEASURE, AND WEALTH
Moses made a conscious choice for righteousness. In so doing, he turned his back on earthly fame, pleasure, and wealth.

> By faith Moses, when he had grown up, refused to be known as the son of Pharaoh's daughter. He chose to be mistreated along with the people of God rather than to enjoy the pleasures of sin for a short time. He regarded disgrace for the sake of Christ as of greater value than the treasures of Egypt, because he was looking ahead to his reward (Heb. 11:24-26).

Righteousness may cost. Prestige in the world's terms often requires the compromise of biblical standards. I know of men who will climb no further on the corporate ladder because of righteous choices in regard to their family and their ethics. Sadly, others have abandoned righteousness to find acclaim. Christian performers, ministers, and evangelists are not exempt. It's tempting to compromise convictions for a broader hearing . . . for a step into the world's spotlight where the applause is easily heard.

Righteousness also demands that we give up the pleasures of sin. Righteousness calls us to invest our lives in the long-term gain of what is right. This is not to say that righteousness does not have its rewards. They are, however, most often long-term. A friend once told me that victory over a particular sin was hard because he enjoyed the sin so much. This confused him. It shouldn't have. Even worms taste good to fish that are about to be caught.

Wealth may be limited because of righteousness. Loss of access to the treasures of Egypt (which we know now were awesome), was the result of Moses' choice to cast his lot with God's people. Loss of corporate mobility, hence, loss of financial gain may be the price. Righteousness means that we give generously to God's kingdom work, which may mean that we have less to spend personally. I often wonder how many young people refuse to explore career ministry opportunities because they don't want to give up the prospects of a financially rewarding career.

It is a tragic and shallow statement about the worth of righteousness when we trade it for a nameplate on the office door, a headline, destructive pleasure, bank accounts, and the things that they provide.

We must hasten to note that righteousness may not preclude fame, pleasure, and wealth. But when Moses had to make a choice, he valued righteousness more than these lesser, fleeting commodities of our world.

Not only did Moses suffer the loss of prestige, pleasure, and wealth, but his righteous choice meant that he would be mistreated along with the people of God. Rejecting fame, pleasure, and wealth for righteousness will leave us vulnerable to be misunderstood and maligned—even at times by our brothers and sisters in Christ.

FEELINGS OF VULNERABILITY

A young woman, going through a crisis experience with her husband, determined to respond righteously. She felt vulnerable. She feared he would take advantage of her and mistreat her more vigorously. Even her Christian friends told her she was foolish "to be so nice" when she was being treated so badly.

David found himself being unjustly discarded from the throne by his son Absalom. Absalom then pursued his father into the wilderness to secure the throne by taking David's life. David chose, at that point, to make righteousness, not safety, his highest goal. He prayed:

> Set a guard over my mouth, O Lord; keep watch over the door of my lips. Let not my heart be drawn to what is evil, to take part in wicked deeds with men who are evildoers; let me not eat of their delicacies. Let a righteous man strike me—it is a kindness; let him rebuke me—it is oil on my head. My head will not refuse it. Yet my prayer is ever against the deeds of evildoers (Ps. 141:3-5).

When we have been treated unrighteously, our first response is to be unrighteous in return. After all, "He did it to me, didn't he?" *Do unto others as they have done unto you* is our tarnished rule. Paul commands, "Do not repay anyone evil for evil. Be careful to do what is right in the eyes of everybody" (Rom. 12:17).

The psalmist writes:

> Do not fret because of evil men or be envious of those who do wrong. . . . Be still before the Lord and wait patiently for Him; do not fret when men succeed in their ways, when they carry out their wicked schemes. Refrain from anger and turn from wrath; do not fret—it leads only to evil. For

evil men will be cut off, but those who hope in the
Lord will inherit the land (Ps. 37:1, 7-9).

Though a choice to be righteous under stress will make us
sense that we are vulnerable and unprotected and as such will
create some additional pain, it will be pain that is ultimately
productive.

DOES RIGHTEOUSNESS PAY?

An associate of mine was scheduled to perform a wedding
with the minister who had been negative toward the former
parishioner who had come to talk with him about her faith in
Christ. As the ministers shared together, the rector began to
ask questions about our ministry and to lament that some of
his people had taken their "spiritual pilgrimage" elsewhere.
My associate soon discovered that his custodial staff all knew
the Lord and had witnessed several times to the rector.

As the rector shared in the wedding, he was impressed
with the sensitive strength in which the Gospel was proclaimed. He remarked about how unique it was that this
couple wanted a Christ-centered home. The next Sunday he
preached about the need for his church members to receive
Christ personally.

The unfailing affirmation of righteous worship around
him had begun to penetrate his heart. Righteousness pays.
Not always in pleasant ways, not always quickly—but it
pays. Christ had to die because of His righteousness. The
dividends have been reaped in millions who have been saved
from the wrath to come and received eternal life.

For the martyrs of the church, their righteous worship

paid off in an early graduation to all that is "far better" and on earth an explosion of church growth that changed the history of the world.

I was sitting alone in a restaurant when the waitress came to pour my coffee. She asked, "Did you see that? That family over there just bowed their heads and said grace." Her voice quieted as she said reflectively, "I grew up in a family where we used to say grace. It's been a long time."

I couldn't help but wonder if that prayer wasn't a reminder that God would use to draw her back to Him. Perhaps an answer to a mother's long-standing prayer. It may have been a small thing, but there was unique power in that public affirmation of righteous worship.

As Ron relocates his family and finds a new job, his righteousness may very well pay off in being placed right where God will use him dramatically. After all, that's what God did with Joseph. Joseph's displacement for righteousness was God's perfect placement.

Moses traded fame, pleasure, and fortune for a significant place in God's program to provide a Messiah, a Saviour for you and me.

I have helped many who have been treated unrighteously. Those who have claimed righteousness as their goal have been paid the dividends of inner peace, a blameless life, a clear conscience, and a testimony that will last into the next generation. Often, their righteousness has drawn their adversary to repentance and led to a restored relationship.

Most importantly, in righteousness we reflect the likeness of Christ. Peter teaches us that Christ suffered unjustly and in so doing gave us an example that we should follow in His steps. In the face of great opposition He did no sin, refused to be deceitful, did not retaliate, and made no threats. Instead He trusted Himself to His Father who is the just judge (1 Peter 2:21-25).

Is it any wonder then that our righteousness brings special pleasure to the Father (1 Peter 2:20) and a special reward at the judgment seat of Christ? (2 Tim. 4:8) Righteousness, though sometimes painful, is always productive.

As we choose righteousness, we become tools in the hand of God. Tools to convict. Tools to draw men to the light. Tools to convince others of the difference between right and wrong. Tools to accomplish the outworking of God's overall plan. Righteousness places us in a usable position.

In our commitment to righteousness, we must never permit self-righteousness to rob our righteousness of its power. Righteousness must be exercised in the context of true humility. We must constantly pray with David, "Search me, O God, and know my heart. . . . See if there is any offensive way in me, and lead me in the way everlasting" (Ps. 139:23-24). If we become proud in our righteousness, we will be powerless as people find offense in our attitude.

GOD'S LAST CHAPTER

Trouble from righteousness sets the stage for God's power and victory. It's like a book with a good ending. The beginning is a story of choices. In the middle the plot thickens and much seems confusing, unfair, and hard. Don't put the book down! Read the last chapter. Our best chapter may be just ahead or in eternity. But it is always a chapter of victory and joy. As it is said of Christ, "For the joy set before Him endured the cross, scorning its shame" (Heb. 12:2).

David knew of God's last chapter when he affirmed:

> I was young and now I am old, yet I have never seen the righteous forsaken or their children begging bread. They are always generous and lend freely; their children will be blessed. Turn from evil and do good; then you will always live securely. For the Lord loves the just and will not forsake His faithful ones. . . . Wait for the Lord and keep His way. He will exalt you to possess the land; when the wicked are cut off, you will see it. I have seen a wicked and ruthless man flourishing like a green tree in its native soil, but he soon passed away and was no more; though I looked for him, he could not be found. Consider the blameless, observe the upright; there is a future for the man of peace. But all sinners will be destroyed; the future of the wicked will be cut off. The salvation of the righteous comes from the Lord; He is their stronghold in time of trouble. The Lord helps them and delivers them; He delivers them from the wicked and saves them, because they take refuge in Him (Ps. 37:25-28, 34-40).

5

RESTORATION
The Trouble with Disobedience

A choice to sin brings trouble. Words are insufficient to describe the magnitude and the terribleness of sin. Sin is terrible in the scope of God's glory. It is devastating in terms of precious relationships. It is profound in its impact on self and our heritage for generations to come. There is nothing more degenerating, more devastating, more awesome in the outpouring of its consequences. Nothing more wrenching, more debilitating than sin.

It should be enough that we are born in sin and we struggle with its alluring ways. But what is incredulous is that we often—with all of our senses intact—*choose* to sin.

Willful sin is self-imposed pain. It is a choice for certain difficulty. Unlike the trouble that comes from righteousness, a choice to sin is an entrance into a degenerative life experience. It is the rape of our souls and the emasculation of our spirits. It is the graffiti on God's glory written in our own hand.

If we are to understand the process and purpose of pain, we must have in clear focus the dynamics of the pain that comes when we choose to sin. A choice to sin brings double trouble, a twofold impact that is as sure as the sin itself.

CONSEQUENCE

The first trouble resulting from sin is *inevitable consequence*.

When God first warned Adam and Eve about their choice to sin, He clearly warned of consequence: "For when you eat of it you will surely die" (Gen. 2:17). Satan's strategy was to contradict the warning. In essence, he said there was no consequence: "You will not surely die" (3:4).

Satan's lies continue today:

Everybody else gets away with it.
It's alright if it doesn't hurt anyone else.
If it feels good, do it.

And so we take the chance. We think, *I can get away with it too. I'll be too clever to let it hurt me. I'll control it, keep it in bounds. I'll stop after I do it just one more time.*

But there is no such thing as taking a chance with sin. The odds are always 100 percent against us. The consequences are inevitable. "You may be sure that your sin will find you out" (Num. 32:23).

Adam and Eve sinned and lost. Their consequences earned the same dividends that sin does today. The first consequence they experienced was *impact*. Sin always has an impact, not only on ourselves, but on others as well. Eve gave to Adam and he ate (Gen. 3:6).

We've all heard that there are some sins you can commit with no effect on others. Not true. Sins committed in the closets of our lives always spill out into the hallways of our existence. Sin changes us. It brings into our existence guilt, fear, and suspicion. That influences how we respond to life and to others.

I recently heard from a friend telling me of his college roommate who was a hemophiliac. Through a recent blood transfusion, his roommate had contracted AIDS, a disease that is spread through promiscuous sexual activity. Only a miracle could save him. It would be hard to tell him that private sins between consenting adults have no impact on others.

Add to impact the *loss of self-esteem* (3:7), *the death of personal integrity* (v. 7), *broken fellowship with God* (v. 8), *fear* (v. 10), and *the surrender of a sense of personal responsibility* (vv. 12-13). The treachery of sin is apparent.

As we move into Genesis 4, Cain sins and in his refusal to repent becomes *angry* with God and with his brother Abel (4:5). The anger from sin actually changed his countenance.

The inevitable consequence of a continuing *struggle with sin* is seen in God's warning to Cain. "If you do not do what is right, sin is crouching at your door; it desires to have you, but you must master it" (v. 7). Once a sin habit begins to develop, we become troubled with the struggle to overcome it. Some people struggle all their lives to keep from falling back into sin's net. For some, the struggle becomes a major distraction of life.

"Cain rose up against Abel his brother, and slew him"

(v. 8, KJV). *Vengeance and harm* accompany our choices to sin. We often lash out against others, perhaps against those who are righteous. We are prone to criticize others for their lifestyles. That makes us feel better about ours. We may even try to silence righteous voices through intimidation, threats, and gossip.

Suspicion adds difficulty to Cain's experience (v. 14). Sin makes us paranoid. Those who cheat in business are always suspicious that others will cheat them. Unfaithful marriage partners suspect their spouses of the same. Sin handcuffs our freedom to interact with people and the world around us in a spirit of trust and confidence.

Lot's selfish choice of the best land in a wicked environment cost him his family. King Saul's repeated rebellion against God cost him the throne and brought a terrible insecurity that manifested itself in anger, jealousy, fear, emotional bondage, and attempted murder. Judas' high priority on comfort and cash led him to hate himself and his 30 pieces of silver, and ultimately, to kill himself.

Sin is a bucketful of suffering looking for a place to be dumped. Recently a friend of mine got a call that the wedding he was preparing to attend had been canceled. The day before the wedding, the groom had sent flowers to a former girlfriend with a note that said, "I still love you."

Distraught, the girl's mother called the priest who was to perform the wedding ceremony and told of the flowers her daughter had received. The priest, on contacting the bride's family, encouraged them to call off the wedding. They did.

Since the engagement ring was a family heirloom, the groom's family wanted it back. The mother and brother of the bride agreed to return the ring. Soon after they arrived at the groom's home, words flared. The groom punched the bride's mother in the face and her son retaliated. A fight ensued and the groom's father stepped in to break it up. In the struggle, he suffered a massive coronary attack and died.

All of that for an unfaithful and disloyal choice to affirm continuing love to an old girlfriend. Who would have ever thought? Sin always causes trouble—even a careless sin.

The ultimate consequence of sin is the *judgment of God* (3:14-19; 4:9-12). Unless we have been justified by Christ, the day will come when we will say, "My punishment is more than I can bear" (4:13). (See John 3:36 and Romans 5:1-10.)

Not only are the consequences of sin inevitable, they are often irreversible. Esau wept with bitter tears, but he could not reclaim what he had lost (Gen. 27:30-40). Judas could not shake the sorrow, so he killed himself (Matt. 27:3-5). Sin leaves us less than we were before, often never to be the same again on earth. Our willful sin is not only hurtful, but also selfish. It not only troubles us with irreversible consequences, but it often leaves a litter of humpty-dumpty lives and relationships that rarely can be mended.

Even forgiveness won't erase some consequences. I have friends who live with flashbacks from years of drug abuse. Homes may stay broken because of sin. Friendships, though forgiveness has been applied, may never be the same. As the poet said so well, "The saddest words of tongue or pen? 'What might have been!' "

We have long claimed 1 John 1:9 and even at times used it as a premeditated "fire escape" for willful sin. While the verse is wonderfully true, we need to remind ourselves that

"God cannot be mocked. A man reaps what he sows. The one who sows to please his sinful nature, from that nature will reap destruction" (Gal. 6:7-8).

DISCIPLINE

My preschool son had been purposefully disobeying as we were enjoying an evening at a friend's house. After clear warning, I took my son by the hand into an obscure bedroom down the hall. I sat on the edge of the bed and said to him, "Look at me."

As fast as I said it, he looked away toward the floor. It was a meditated act of rebellion. A test of who was really in charge.

Now the issue was not what had happened in the living room, but the rebellion in the bedroom. My son's choice to rebel brought difficulty as he repeated his downward glance after two spankings. Finally, after the third, when I said, "Now look at me," he opened his eyes wide and riveted his attention on my face.

The difficulty imposed on him was not intended to "punish" him. It was the only way a loving father could draw attention to rebellion and reroute the son's life to obedience. The discipline won the day for what was right.

That's exactly what God's discipline is like. His discipline does what is necessary to capture our attention and put us back in the ways of righteousness.

Sin will bring the difficulty of discipline. While not *all* difficulty is discipline, all dicipline *is* difficult. And discipline is the second inevitable part of the double trouble that comes from sin.

Initially, for the believer, God's discipline is not punitive. God punished us at the cross. We do not stand in double jeopardy before God. God's discipline is corrective. He will put just enough pressure on us to move us back into His fellowship. Discipline is redemptive. Restorative. That's why Paul encourages the Corinthian believers to correct themselves so that they won't have to be corrected by God (1 Cor. 11:31-32).

If we are God's children we can expect to be disciplined.

> Endure hardship as discipline; God is treating you as sons. For what son is not disciplined by his father? If you are not disciplined (and everyone undergoes discipline), then you are illegitimate children and not true sons. Moreover, we have all had human fathers who disciplined us and we respected them for it. How much more should we submit to the Father of our spirits and live! (Heb. 12:7-9)

God disciplines His own. If we are not disciplined by God, then we are illegitimate children.

God disciplines us because He loves us. "Do not despise the Lord's discipline and do not resent His rebuke, because the Lord disciplines those He loves, as a father the son he delights in" (Prov. 3:11-12). God's love does not mean that He always likes or approves of what we do, but rather that He intensely cares for us. He cares enough to pressure us back to safety.

God disciplines us internally (Ps. 32:1-4). After David sinned with Bathsheba, he felt God's inner pursuits.

When I kept silent, my bones wasted away
through my groaning all day long. For day and
night Your hand was heavy upon me; my strength
was sapped as in the heat of summer. Then I
acknowledged my sin to You and did not cover up
my iniquity. I said, "I will confess my transgres-
sions to the Lord"—and You forgave the guilt of
my sin (Ps. 32:3-5).

By David's own admission, he groaned within. His inner
strength was gone. God's Spirit shouts within us as we try to
keep our sins silent. C.S. Lewis wrote in *The Problem of Pain,*
"God whispers to us in our pleasures, speaks to us in our
conscience and shouts to us in our pain."

God disciplines us externally (Jonah 1). As God had to
ultimately use Nathan as an external instrument in David's
repentance, so it was with Jonah. Jonah, however, was so at
peace with himself that he slept like a baby, even in a terrible
storm. There are times when we have so rationalized our
sins that our fig leaves muffle any internal discipline.

God pursued Jonah externally. God sovereignly nudged
Jonah back with a storm, a pagan sea captain, dice that
pointed the finger at him, and the awkwardness of having to
give a public testimony in the midst of his sin. But Jonah
would rather die than obey God so he was thrown over-
board. God disciplined him with a fish.

I love the story of Jonah. It demonstrates that God has
options of discipline that we've never dreamed of. Watch for
His external, sovereign nudges on your life. A friend, a
sermon, communion, public exposure, a reproof of life. In
increasing intensity, God will press you back to Himself. It

may be painful and unpleasant, but it will always be productive.

God disciplines us persistently. Jonah proves that God persists in discipline. As a parent, I have on occasion felt like giving up in disciplining my children. But God never quits.

DEALING WITH THE DIFFICULTY OF WILLFUL SIN

God's purpose in communicating concerning consequence to us is that it might serve as a fair and real warning to avoid the trauma of sin. A commitment to be *decidedly righteous* is the best way to avoid the difficulty of sin. To be forewarned is to be forearmed in our battle against the adversary.

God's purpose in discipline is to draw us back in *effective repentance*. Effective repentance in the place of stubborn resistance is the only solution in discipline. Effective repentance is a turning, a changing of direction. It consists of seven steps.

1. *Admit and agree.* David admitted his sin and agreed with God that it was wrong. We are often able to admit our sin, but want to discount how wrong it may have been. Before a holy God, our wrongs are clearly wrong. We must see our sin from His point of view (Ps. 32:5; 1 John 1:9).

2. *Submit to God's leadership.* Immediately we must yield our will and spirit for God's direction. This is unconditional surrender. David closes his psalm of repentance with a call from God to submission in the days ahead (Ps. 32:8-10).

3. *Rejoice in forgiveness.* Now we are clean. God forgives. Rejoice! Praise Him in prayer, song, and public testimony (vv. 1-2, 11).

How, in repentance, can you build resistance to future sin?

4. *Rekindle your knowledge of God and draw near to Him.* In

Psalm 139 David meditates on God's omnipresence and intimate omniscience of him as a person. The wonder of this knowledge drives David into a close relationship with God. His awareness of the greatness of God moves him from ritual to reality in his worship. As the psalmist says, "The fear of the Lord is the beginning of wisdom" (Ps. 111:10).

5. *Identify with God's passion against sin.* A tolerant, permissive attitude toward sin leaves us vulnerable. God hates sin. Fellowship with God means that without establishing myself as a judge of others, I hate what He hates and love what He loves. I grieve over what His heart grieves about. I rejoice in what He rejoices in (Ps. 139:19-22). This emotional identity with God positionalizes me as an enemy of sin and a friend of righteousness.

6. *Maintain a humble transparency before God.* In his passion against sin, David realized that he could not have a self-righteous attitude, but needed the incisive inspection of God Himself. He prayed, "Search me, O God, and know my heart; test me and know my anxious thoughts. See if there is any offensive way in me, and lead me in the way everlasting" (Ps. 139:23-24). We must invite the divine inspector into every corner of our lives. Every thought. Every word. Every relationship. Every attitude.

7. *Glorify God in the consequences that remain.* Though the remaining consequences of sin are painful, they always can be used for good. The sorrow resulting from our sin serves as a regular reminder of the awfulness of that sin. It is a buffer zone between your life and sin. As 2 Corinthians 7:10 teaches, godly sorrow brings repentance. As long as the sorrow is there, the freedom to recommit the sin will be chained.

Memories of the sin can be a springboard to praise. Each time a confessed sin is remembered, break into praise and thanksgiving for the forgiveness that God has given. Thank Him for your cleanness in Christ. Memories can stimulate us to pray for others who are facing similar temptations. We should also pray for those injured because of the sin and for increased strength for ourselves to become more like Christ.

God is able to bring beauty even from the ashes of our sin as we become decidedly righteous and effectively repentant for His glory.

May God help us to passionately hate sin and may He find our hearts ready to be led in the way everlasting.

SUFFICIENCY
Who Needs God?

Recently a friend asked if the affluence of our church members was a problem. My guess was that he suspected that a lot of our members were caught up in materialism and in striving for gain. While that may be true for some, that's not our worst problem. Our struggle in affluence is that we lose sight of how much we need God.

Sensing our need for God is tough. Knowing that we need Him gets lost in the fact that we have all we need. Clothes, food, safety, security, friendship, and fun are all readily available.

Assuming that we have provided it all for ourselves, we become self-sufficient. Self-sufficiency is a curse because it blocks out God. When we cease to perceive how much we need God, He soon seems out of sight, then out of mind, then out of life.

This is a problem for all Americans. We live in an affluent

and all-providing culture. If we can't afford something, we buy it on credit. If we are poor, we rely on government aid. We have our health, houses, families, jobs, friends, and heritage. Who needs God?

In his work, *The Problem of Pain,* C.S. Lewis wrote, "Everyone has noticed how hard it is to turn our thoughts to God when everything is going well. The statement, 'we have all we want,' is a terrible statement if that all does not include God." He goes on to cite St. Augustine who said, "God wants to give us something but He cannot. Our hands are full and there is nowhere to put anything."

The tragedy of this self-sufficiency is that it is deceitful. We end up placing our trust in our money, family, job, income, friends, and our own ingenuity as though they will last forever. They are all fleeting; each could be gone in a moment. God is the only steady, daily, eternal reality that is sufficient for all our needs and wants.

THE JEOPARDY OF SELF-SUFFICIENCY

Self-sufficiency distorts our responses to life. When our sufficiency is in earthly things, we are tempted to manipulate, intimidate, or compromise our righteousness to maintain our false sense of security.

Self-sufficiency leads to pride and self-glory. Pride and self-glory are repulsive to God. They are the ultimate consequences of a self-sufficient life.

Christ reproved the church at Laodicea. "You say, 'I am rich; I have acquired wealth and do not need a thing.' But you do not realize that you are wretched, pitiful, poor, blind and naked" (Rev. 3:17).

Self-sufficiency leads as well to idolatry. We end up worshiping those things which provide our sufficiency and security. If that source is not God, then we will cease to worship God. Whatever the false source of our sufficiency may be—whether it be a husband, a wife, a child, a job, a brilliant mind, good health, or happiness—it will soon take first place in our lives.

God, knowing that self-sufficiency turns to pride and idolatry, warned Israel about their entrance into the Promised Land.

> When the Lord your God brings you into the land He swore to your fathers, to Abraham, Isaac and Jacob, to give you—a land with large, flourishing cities you did not build, houses filled with all kinds of good things you did not provide, wells you did not dig, and vineyards and olive groves you did not plant—then when you eat and are satisfied, be careful that you do not forget the Lord, who brought you out of Egypt, out of the land of slavery (Deut. 6:10-12).

Sure enough, the Israelites went into the land of plenty and forgot the Lord.

Often the only way the Lord can accomplish a sense of God-sufficiency in us is to strip away the layers of our self-sufficiency. That stripping may be painful.

Let me tell you about a self-sufficient woman. She worked for a wealthy couple. They saw to it that she had all she needed—clothes, food, and security. She had a son. He was the joy of her life. She had heard about God, but she didn't *need* Him. He was little more than a word in her vocabulary.

Suddenly, difficulty stripped her life of *everything*. All she had was gone. All, that is, but God.

COMING TO THE END OF OURSELVES

Hagar's story begins in Genesis 16 when she bears a son to Abraham. Hagar is the head maidservant of Sarah, Abraham's wife. According to cultural custom, if there was no heir through the wife, the chief woman servant was to bear the heir. Hagar did, and named her son Ishmael.

Now the problems begin. Expelled once from her home because of Sarah's anger, God met Hagar and sent her back. In time, God opened Sarah's womb and she bore the legitimate heir of God's promises to Abraham. As brothers are prone to do, Ishmael taunted and mocked young Isaac. Sarah, seeing her son being mocked, demanded that Abraham get rid of Ishmael and Hagar.

Note that Hagar's difficulty is not self-induced. In fact, she was a victim of Abraham and Sarah's scheme. Since Hagar was a slave, she had no choice but to bear Abraham's child. Later, she was a victim of her son's behavior. Finally, she was a victim of Abraham's decision. While simply doing her duty and living life responsibly, Hagar's life fell apart.

More significantly, Hagar's difficulty is God ordained. God says to Abraham, "Do not be so distressed about the boy and your maidservant. Listen to whatever Sarah tells you, because it is through Isaac that your offspring will be reckoned" (Gen. 21:12). This was not ordained of God because God doesn't care about servants and loved Sarah best. God always has a fair, just, and good reason for what

He ordains. There was a reason beyond Hagar's comprehension.

God's Messiah seed was in jeopardy. God promised that the seed of woman would someday strike a fatal blow to the domain of Satan (Gen. 3:15). That promise was renewed to Abraham. Isaac would carry on the Messiah seed. The story of Cain and Abel demonstrates that Satan will do all he can to extinguish the righteous seed that may fulfill God's promise and threaten his existence. Lest the story of Cain and Abel be repeated at that point in history, God sovereignly intervened. Isaac and Ishmael are separated to secure the safety of the Messianic promise to Isaac. This separation not only serves the purposes of God's Messianic plan, but it is used by God to accomplish a significant work in Hagar's life.

Victimized by circumstances in a problem ordained by God, Hagar now sees her life go from bad to worse. Stripped away are her privileges as the chief maidservant— her fine garments, her food, her security, and her health. All that she had was reduced now to a boy, some bread, a bottle, and a wilderness (21:14).

God is in the process of removing the layers of Hagar's self-sufficiency. Some of us can identify. Hagar loses her *purpose* in life (v. 14). She goes from a maidservant to a nomad. Caretaker of a wealthy estate to manager of dwindling provisions.

Hagar loses her *provisions* for life (v. 15). Soon the water and the bread are spent; thirst and hunger replace them.

Hagar loses her *prized possession* (16:6-16). There was only one thing that was of deep personal worth to Hagar—her son, Ishmael. She now abandons him because she can't bear the agony of watching him die.

Can you walk in Hagar's shoes? Can you sense her help-less despair? Ration out the last few sips of water as they pass your lips under the intense heat of the sun. Think of the agony of losing the glory of your past position, security, and comfort. Watch as the young boy grows weaker in the wilderness. A boy not yet hardened to the rigors of life. Weakening, failing, groaning in pain, dying.

Hagar has lost everything. She has come to the end of herself.

I can't help but cry, "Where is God?" Is His hand with-ered that He cannot help? Is His heart hardened that He will not weep with her? Are His ears deaf that He cannot hear her cries? Is He not there? Is He so cruel as to ordain a difficulty that would waste and destroy?

AT THE END OF OURSELVES . . .GOD

Hagar's setting is by God's design. He has designed that the layers of her *sufficiency* be stripped away so that He might rebuild her life with *His sufficiency*. When Hagar comes to the end of herself, God is there.

Hagar needed a firsthand experience with God. She need-ed to know the reality of God. That God loved *her*. That God would supply for *her*. That He could be *her* sufficiency.

At best, Hagar had a secondhand relationship with God. Though God briefly met her in Genesis 16:13, she primarily knew God as the God of Abraham and Sarah. She had watched *their* God work for *them* and supply miraculously for *them*. Their God would now become her God. Dramati-cally, He would personalize Himself to her. It required first that she be reduced to nothingness so that God could prove

His sufficiency.

He provides Hagar with a personal experience with *God's Word*.

> God heard the boy crying, and the angel of God called to Hagar from heaven and said to her, "What is the matter, Hagar? Do not be afraid; God has heard the boy crying as he lies there. Lift the boy up and take him by the hand, for I will make him into a great nation."
> Then God opened her eyes and she saw a well of water. So she went and filled the skin with water and gave the boy a drink (Gen. 21:17-19).

God now gives Hagar His *peace* in the place of her fear (v. 17). He provides a *personal promise*. He grants to her a new *future*, a new *purpose* for life (v. 18). God demonstrates that He will be her *provider*, miraculously when necessary (v. 19).

Many of us have secondhand relationships with God. We have sung everyone else's hymns. We have echoed the reverent prayers and praises of others. We have hitchhiked on everyone else's faith. We have lived on our religious heritage. Tragically, these are all empty and bankrupt experiences if they have not led to a firsthand, intimate relationship with Christ.

Our problem is that we don't realize how desperately we need God. We have all we need and want; we are satisfied with our lives. So God pursues us to bring us to our senses spiritually, to reduce us to the heights of knowing Him personally and intimately.

EXPERIENCING GOD

As it was with Hagar, at the end of yourself God's Word will begin to speak to you personally. Passages that were often nice but remote will anchor themselves in your heart with a deep sense of significance. You can expect God's promises to become personal realities to which you cling in the swift torrent of trouble. When difficulties have demolished your dreams, God will give you a new dream—His dream for you. You can expect God to provide, perhaps dramatically. For you there will be a well in the wilderness; an ending in which all things have worked together for good. In it all you will come to know the Lord as your God. As Hagar said in her first encounter with God, "You are the God who sees *me*" (Gen. 16:13).

Gideon needed to know and demonstrate the sufficiency of God. When he came against the Midianites, God instituted a troop "build down" proposal. The army was reduced to 300 men. Why? So that Israel would not falsely boast in their own power (Jud. 7:2). The Israelites needed to know the power of God firsthand, that God alone is sufficient. All God needed at Midian was 300 witnesses.

David came against Goliath as a young man. Saul offered David the sufficiency of his armor (1 Sam. 17:38-39). Saul was large; he stood head and shoulders above everyone else (9:2). In Saul's armor David would have taken two steps before the armor moved. Saul's sufficiency would have gotten in David's way.

David knew the sufficiency of God. He said to Saul, "The Lord who delivered me from the paw of the lion and the paw of the bear will deliver me from the hand of this Philistine" (17:37). David refused to walk around in anyone else's armor and was personally victorious in the sufficiency of God.

There were times in the early part of our ministry when our income fell short of our expenses, times when there was too much month left at the end of the money. That was difficult for us. It was troubling to see others who were prospering. It was a struggle to park our old beat-up car next to shiny up-to-date models.

But God was in it all. At the beginning of our married life and ministry, God wanted to teach me and my wife something very central to our faith: His sufficiency to meet all our needs. So He stripped away our sufficiency and faithfully, miraculously at times, met *every* single need. He clothed us. He supplied for us. He personally cared for us. I wouldn't trade what we learned as a family about our God for anything. But God had to reduce my ability to make money to show us His love and power.

Debbie Jackson Searles was a student and a part of that first church we pastored. She was a happy, helpful person. Friends often came to her for counsel and encouragement. Then, surprisingly, Deb went through a confusing crisis that left her severely depressed. Unable to climb out of it, she was ultimately hospitalized. In time the doctors diagnosed a problem with her body chemistry and, with proper medication, were able to restore her to her original vitality.

She told me later that God had tailor-made that trauma for her. As she said, "I was not living in any 'big' sin, but God needed to purge out a growing sense of pride and self-sufficiency. I needed to be aware of His presence and place in my life."

Deb left that crisis with a new song in her heart. I'll never forget hearing Christine Wyrtzen sing the song that Debbie wrote. I listened. The words pierced my heart:

> I've been through a fire
>   That has deepened my desire
> To know the living God more and more.
>   It hasn't been much fun,
> But the work that it has done
>   In my life has made it worth the hurt.
> You see, sometimes we need the hard times
>   To bring us to our knees,
> Otherwise we do as we please and never heed Him.
>   But He always knows what's best,
> And it's when we are distressed
>   That we really come to know God as He is.

Don was a top executive in the prime of his career. A heart attack and an ensuing stroke left him unable to remember basic everyday things. But Don has come through this crisis time with a new and fresh touch of the Lord. He talks more now about how much he loves the Lord, how he has finally sensed God's personal reality in his life. Don takes the initiative to pray with his wife about things that they never prayed about before. He is more sensitive to his family now with a new warmth and tenderness. God cracked Don's shell and began a significant work in his life. When Don's own significance was gone, things of true significance could come to the fore.

It's no wonder that the psalmist declares:

> Whom have I in heaven but You? And being with
> You, I desire nothing on earth. My flesh and my

heart may fail, but God is the strength of my heart and my portion forever (Ps. 73:25-26).

BLOOM WHERE PLANTED

Often, when crisis reduces our sufficiency, we will be totally changed and a new life situation will emerge. It was that way for Hagar. She could not return to Abraham and Sarah. Ishmael would marry. Hagar would begin a new life. She bloomed where she was planted.

Don't look back. Don't long for past comfort and security. God knows that if we go back, we may become self-sufficient again. Be productive in God's place for you.

When God uses pain to bring you to the end of yourself, He will meet you there. He will be there with His Word for you, His certain promises, His provisions.

God knows that the only sufficiency that is truly sufficient in life is the sufficiency of Himself. So He works until He has us singing:

> I need Thee every hour
>   In joy or pain;
> Come quickly and abide,
>   Or life is vain.
>
> I need Thee, oh I need Thee,
>   Ev'ry hour I need Thee!
> O bless me now, my Savior,
>   I come to Thee!
>   ANNIE S. HAWKS

7

RISK REDUCTION
The Productivity of Thorns

Insecure?

I would have never guessed it of him. He was a well-known communicator, an effective teacher of the Word. And now he was telling his congregation that he often felt insecure. I was surprised, but I could identify with the feeling.

I, too, find insecurity a frequent companion. It gnaws at me and internally humbles me. It plagues my heart with questions. Did I preach an effective sermon? Was I misunderstood? Will that special person accept me for what I am? What am I doing here? Shouldn't I be better as a father? Am I as sensitive as I should be to my wife?

To be straightforward, I dislike insecure feelings intensely. But as much as I dislike their intrusion into my life, I realize that they have tremendous value. Value to God and value to my productivity for Him. When I am feeling insecure, my heart flies to the Lord for strength. I seek Him for perspective; I search His Word for comfort. Not only does insecurity keep me close to God, but it keeps me from unfounded pride. It reminds me of how truly insufficient I am in and of myself. It reminds me of how much I need God. My insecurities make me sensitive to others.

I have come to realize that I am a risk to God's effective work through me. Pride, insensitivity, self-sufficiency, and a host of other potential risks lurk under the surface of my life.

Pride chokes my productivity by alienating those whom God wants to reach through me. Pride leaves the door of my life open to many failures. A door through which lying, moral impurity, stubbornness, anger, and vengeance can walk. I know as well that self-sufficiency produces the works of God in the strength of my human abilities. This leaves me nonproductive and vulnerable to glorying in myself. Insensitivity leads me to ignore the needs of others who hurt and leads me primarily to a selfish perspective in life.

My insecurity serves to reduce the risk of pride, self-sufficiency, and insensitivity. It turns pride into genuine humility, self-sufficiency into a trust in God to be sufficient for me, and my insensitivity into a useful and empathetic sensitivity to others.

Thorns reduce the risk to God's work through us and yield us as productive servants of Christ.

RISK REDUCTION
Risk reduction is not uncommon to us. We take a lot of measures to protect things precious to us. We are willing to take phenomenal steps to reduce the risks to our lives,

health, money, friends, power, and prestige.

Soon after the "Tylenol" deaths in the early 1980s, Tylenol marketed their pills in tamper-proof, sealed bottles with this statement in plain view: DO NOT USE IF THE SEAL IS BROKEN. Laws have recently been passed forcing us to use our seat belts. Exorbitant amounts of money are paid for insurance against theft or loss. Home security systems are installed. We enroll in self-defense courses. We eat right and get enough sleep to guard our health. All of this to reduce risks.

God runs a phenomenal risk when He entrusts His work and reputation to us. His reputation in this world is largely seen through those of us who claim to be His children. Yet we are prone to bouts of pride, selfishness, moral impurity, jealousy, anger, and a host of other diseases. We still, as the stewards of God's kingdom work, are risks to Him. He trusts us to train the next generation for His glory. He trusts us with the proclamation of the great oracles of His truth. He has committed to us the financial support of the ministry of Christ's kingdom. The spreading of the Good News to a lost world has been placed in our hands.

Trusting all of this to us is indeed risky business. God must feel something like my friend did who was giving his daughter in marriage. His daughter was a well-mannered, beautiful young woman. When the groom-to-be came to ask for her hand, my friend admitted that he felt like he was handing over a priceless Stradivarius violin to a 200-pound gorilla.

Is it any wonder that God seeks to reduce the risk of His work through us? Though there are many ways He may do it, for Paul it was through a thorn of difficulty and trouble.

God uses thorns to reduce the risk.

THORNS IN THE FLESH
Second Corinthians 12:7-10 outlines for us the productivity of Paul's risk reducing thorn. Paul relates the problem, purpose, and proper response to the pain of thorns:

> To keep me from becoming conceited because of these surpassingly great revelations, there was given me a thorn in my flesh, a messenger of Satan, to torment me. Three times I pleaded with the Lord to take it away from me. But He said to me, "My grace is sufficient for you, for My power is made perfect in weakness." Therefore I will boast all the more gladly about my weaknesses, so that Christ's power may rest on me. That is why, for Christ's sake, I delight in weaknesses, in insults, in hardships, in persecutions, in difficulties. For when I am weak, then I am strong (2 Cor. 12:7-10).

Initially, Paul *recognized his vulnerability*. He knew that pride could be a very real problem for him. He had been the object of God's special attention. God had shared phenomenal revelations with him, revelations not trusted to anyone else (vv. 1-6). He realized that this could lead to a distortion of Paul's self-perception and that his heart could become conceited.

Arrogance is a tremendous barrier to our effectiveness for God. How open are you to arrogant people? Have you ever listened to a proud man attempt to teach you the Word? I find that when I discern a spirit of pride I am tempted to block the teacher out. Pride hinders effective communication and makes effective relationships impossible. Self-exaltation is a risk. It distorts and blocks God's work through us. Paul was wise enough to perceive that his difficulty reduced the risk of pride.

What was Paul's risk reducer? Scripture does not tell us. While it may have been a disfiguration in his eyes (Gal. 4:15), Paul simply indicates that it was a difficulty sent by Satan that was a permanent and troubling condition. The Greek word for thorn, *skolops,* means "a pointed stake." This was a problem of major proportions and, like thorns that are stuck in our bodies, Paul was constantly aware of its presence.

Thorns come in many shapes and sizes. A thorn could be something *physical* as it might have been for Paul. A sickness. A bodily limitation. Or it could be something *emotional.* An insecurity that keeps you close to the Saviour. Charles Haddon Spurgeon, London's greatest preacher of the last generation, often felt heavy weights of despondency that deepened his sensitivity to Christ and the crises of others. It may be the feeling of sorrow that lingers from a past sin and keeps you from committing it again.

A thorn might be *environmental.* A businessman was recently sharing how there seemed to be little possibility of a promotion for him in his company. He related how frustrating that was for him until he realized that it was of God. He shared that he was intense and aggressive in his work and that he had a struggle with materialism. "I'd sell my soul to the company if I was moving up quickly. God has done this to focus my attention on the priorities of my family and my relationship to the Lord. He keeps me from the danger of making my business, money, and things a god in my life."

A thorn could be something *social,* perhaps a person—an in-law or a headstrong child. God has always seen fit to periodically place in my life someone who has been uniquely used of Him to reduce the risk of carelessness, slothfulness, and pride.

Actually, a thorn in the flesh can be anything—anything that reduces the risk in me to hinder God's effective work through me. It is anything that refines me and keeps me sharp for His glory. Anything that keeps pride, arrogance, self-sufficiency, immorality, or any other lust of the flesh in check so that God can work without my getting in the way. A thorn is anything that reduces self and resurrects the power of Christ.

RESPONDING TO THORNS

Paul's thorn was a messenger of Satan. This rings true with our earlier discussion that affirmed Satan as the primary source of pain. It thrills me to watch God turn Satan's best efforts to defeat us (the thorn could have been a source of bitterness and anger for Paul) into usefulness for His glory. God can always use what Satan intends for abuse. The key to that victory is our response.

We can respond by letting the thorn fester to produce a discouragement that leads to bitterness, anger, self-pity, and defeat. Or we can look at our pain from God's point of view and discover its usefulness. Paul's four responses are the keys to his thorn becoming productive in his life.

First, Paul sought *release* (2 Cor. 12:8). He prayed, pleaded with the Lord three times to take the thorn away. It is not to our spiritual credit to want to experience pain. Even Christ asked the Father three times to remove the cup of His suffering. That's where Paul began. He did the most he could to seek release and God answered his prayer. But God's answer was no. In certain circumstances, pain is more productive than release. It was that way for Paul.

When God said no, Paul adjusted. Thorns in the flesh are a lot like stones in your shoes. If you can't get them out, you adjust to them. Though the adjustment may take some time, it is absolutely critical to using your thorns productively.

After seeking release, Paul adjusted by *tapping the resource*—God's grace (v. 9). Grace is God's help to us when we do not deserve it, when we cannot help ourselves. God's grace is available to us through several channels. God's Word is one source of help in trouble. His Word provides comfort, proper mental orientation, promise, and purpose. "If Your Law had not been my delight, I would have perished in my affliction" (Ps. 119:92).

A lady sat in my office and told me of her recent crisis. It was terribly complex and very confusing. It left her full of despair. Few of us could identify with the magnitude of her problem. She said, "Pastor, there have been times when I have lost all support from around me. Times when I felt disoriented and totally alone in my confusion. In those times, all I had was the strength of the Word of God. It was my only stability. The only mark on the compass of my life, my only point of hope and orientation. Pastor, I've made it this far because God's Word is there and God's Word is true." She had experienced the grace of Scripture.

God's grace also comes through prayer. Hebrews 4:16 says, "Let us then approach the throne of grace with confidence, so that we may receive mercy and find grace to help us in our time of need." This kind of praying is more than, "Now I lay me down to sleep," or, "Thanks for the food," or "Give me what I want." This kind of praying stays before God's throne, agonizing if necessary till the grace breaks through. The grace of prayer may be a settling peace that comes over your spirit. It may be God's reminder of a specific promise to which you can cling. As you talk with God, you may be reminded of His mercy, His power to turn that which seems bad into that which is good, His loving care for you, or any other of a dozen qualities of our God. Prayer changes your perspective in times of trouble and blesses you with the grace to bear up victoriously.

Grace also comes to those who reject personal pride and take a humble posture in pain. "God opposes the proud but gives grace to the humble" (1 Peter 5:5). Who are the proud in pain? They are those who demand comfort and ease. Those who think they deserve better. They are those who say, "God, not *me!*" Those who say, "I'll do it alone, Lord, if You don't mind. I'll make it through this by myself."

The proud shake their fists toward heaven and curse God. The proud curdle their spirits with bitterness, blaming God and others for their pain. They choke off the grace that the humble receive.

The humble, like Christ, say, "Yet not as I will, but as You will" (Matt. 26:39). The humble submit to thorns instead of resisting them. They are the ones who receive the grace of God.

God says that grace also comes through the words of those around us. "Do not let any unwholesome talk come out of your mouths, but only what is helpful for building others up according to their needs, that it may benefit [literally, "give grace to"] those who listen" (Eph. 4:29). The carefully chosen words of those in the family of God are a source of God's grace. A word of encouragement. A word of strength. A word of God's perspective. A word of understanding. "A word aptly spoken is like apples of gold in settings of silver" (Prov. 25:11).

After being denied release and adjusting by tapping the source of grace, Paul *realized the purpose of this thorn in his life.* He realized that God's "power is made perfect in weakness" (2 Cor. 12:9). Paul's thorn prevented him from developing a spirit of pride and arrogance; therefore, his thorn enabled God's power to be full and unhindered. The risk had been reduced and God's work was maximized!

I have a dear friend in the ministry. He is handsome, intelligent, and talented. I have never been less than blessed when he breaks the bread of God's Word. He lives with a nervous twitch that causes his whole body to tighten and recoil in a muscle spasm. It happens every couple of minutes—except when he is preaching. Then it is unusually controlled. I am convinced that God uses this thorn to project His strength through him. To reduce the risk of a host of destructive forces that come with such unique and powerful gifts. Paul's thorn enabled him to say, "I can do everything *through* Him who gives me strength" (Phil. 4:13). I wonder if, without the thorn, Paul might have been tempted to say, "*I* can do all things."

Finally, Paul *responded with gladness and delight* (2 Cor. 12:9-10). Paul wanted nothing less than for Christ to be strong through him. If it took trouble to accomplish that goal, then Paul would rejoice in the trouble. He knew that his thorn was a companion to keep his life eternally productive. "For Christ's sake, I delight in weaknesses, in insults, in hardships, in persecutions, in difficulties. For when I am weak, then I am strong" (v. 10).

Upon visiting a church, we took our son Matthew to his Sunday School class. A small, bent over, hunched back lady met us with a glowing smile and a warm welcome for Matt. Later Matthew excitedly told us about what he had learned and what songs his class had sung. We were impressed with the unusual effectiveness of that teacher.

I was soon to become the pastor of that church. I marvelled often at this widow's positive spirit. It was contagious. I'll never forget the day she shared her secret with me. She said, "Pastor, God has made me small and bent over so that I can be right down where children are! I love them so much and if I weren't like this I couldn't relate to them so well." She had turned her thorn into triumph. It was the key to her usefulness. It had become a blessing and she rejoiced in it.

God working through us is risky business. If it takes a thorn for Him to be effective and productive in our lives, then let us tap the grace, realize the purpose, and rejoice.

USABILITY
The Divine Boot Camp

Our newspaper recently carried a story about a clergyman who was not only liberal theologically, but sociologically as well. His sermons regularly carried the theme of the goodness of everyone. Only environments were evil. He sided against the police and often cried out about their brutality. He supported laws that favored the rights of the criminal over the rights of the victim. He cast his lot often with the American Civil Liberties Union in their social action endeavors.

A week before this clergyman was scheduled to speak to his church's senior citizens group, he was mugged by some hoodlums who robbed and beat him mercilessly. He was injured and shaken, both emotionally and philosophically. He nearly cancelled the engagement, but then thought better of it and showed up in bandages and a sling.

As he began his speech, he told how the mugging had

caused him to rethink all of his social positions. He admitted that he had been shaken to the core. To the group's surprise, he said that, in spite of it, he had decided that he would not let that violent episode change his views or his theology. He would go on preaching as he always had. At that point, an old woman in the last row stood up and shouted, "Mug him again!"

WHO NEEDS TO BE CHANGED?

We do.

It's amusing how we go through life feeling that everyone else ought to change—and we know just how it should be done. We act as though we are God's appointed agents of change. It never seems to cross our minds that God may wish to change *us*.

With four years of seminary study in my pocket, I walked into my first ministry with an agenda of ideas as long as my arm. I thought, *I'm here to change this place.* And God said, "Mug him."

The board members in that first church loved me, but they kept my feet to the fire in administrative details. I needed to be changed. I needed to know how to work with lay leadership, how to be careful in my work, how to dream with others. I needed to develop those skills so I would be capable and usable in the days ahead. As unpleasant as it was at the time, it was God's change agent in my life.

Then I assumed that I was ready. Capable. Usable.

I took my next pastorate. I asked all the right questions. I knew everything that should be changed. I could see exactly why God had led me there. Boot camp was behind me. It was *my* turn to be the agent of change. I walked in, ready to go, and it was as though God said, "Mug him again."

And now I'm in Michigan. After nearly four years here, there are a lot of things that have changed in the ministry. But God has used this place to change more things in me than I have been used to change in it.

I often wonder how many times God has to "mug me" before His message gets through. Before I change my mind to think like He thinks. Before He has me in a form and place that I am usable in His kingdom work.

I hasten to say that God really does not mug us. But He does encounter us on the streets of our existence to bring about change in our lives. To change us so that He might use us.

I'm glad God's not finished with me yet. It gives me a sense of confidence to know He cares enough for me to continue to shape, mold, mend, and stretch me. I want to be useful to Him. Though it sometimes hurts, the pain is worth the gain. It is His goal to change us into instruments "useful to the Master and prepared to do any good work" (2 Tim. 2:21).

DAVID

It's hard for us to imagine what happened in this little shepherd boy's heart the day the great prophet of Israel came to his house, passed by all his older brothers, and anointed David as the next king of Israel. If I promised my sons that someday they would play for the world champion Detroit Tigers, they would never forget it. All their years of development would be filled with that anticipation. Multiply that feeling and perhaps you can understand what being king meant to David.

More special yet is that it all began to come true. David was invited to play his harp for King Saul. He became fast friends with Jonathan, the king's son. The women of Israel sang his praises. David was often at the king's house. It all made sense. Someday soon God would make *him* king.

Then in a rage Saul hurled a spear at him. David fled. Soon he was now a fugitive, running for his life. For 10 years David fled, hiding in caves with a band of loyal men. Desperate and deserted, he cried, "How long, O Lord? Will You forget me forever? How long will You hide Your face from me? How long must I wrestle with my thoughts and every day have sorrow in my heart? How long will my enemy triumph over me? Look on me and answer, O Lord my God. Give light to my eyes, or I will sleep in death; my enemy will say, 'I have overcome him' and my foes will rejoice when I fall" (Ps. 13:1-4). The heavens were deafeningly silent.

God needed David to be a warrior, a man of military might and skill. He would lead God's people in conquering Israel's enemies. He would make way for the next king, Solomon, a king of peace, to build the temple.

How do you take a shepherd boy and make him a man of military might and skill? You send him to boot camp for 10 years where he becomes an instant general to a growing band of men. David learned the terrain intimately and knew every cave and corner of the topography. Most importantly, he learned that God was his protector and provider.

As David fled from Saul, his time of trial endeared him to all of Israel. He protected the people's flocks and kept their land safe from Philistine marauders (1 Sam. 25). This developed into a coast-to-coast popularity for David. A grass roots support for him to become king.

Six hundred men gathered themselves to David, men who were the dregs of society (23:13). "Those who were in distress or in debt or discontented gathered around [David], and he became their leader" (22:2).

How do you take a lonely shepherd boy and make him a leader and manager of men? Give him 10 years with 600 unusual men. Then he will be ready to manage the people of Israel.

David was righteous, but not ready. For David, this 10-year ordeal was an extended trial. But for God, it was just long enough to make David capable and usable.

The pattern is clear in Joseph's life as well. The Lord used suffering to place Joseph where He would use him to rescue the Messiah seed from starvation. God used a three-year stint in the slammer to knock off Joseph's arrogance so that he might humbly forgive his brothers (Gen. 37—50). All of this to make a righteous man ready. To make Joseph usable and capable for God.

GOD'S GOAL—CHANGE

James writes to first-century Jewish believers that God wants to use trouble as an agent of change in their lives. Their life situations were fraught with difficulty. First, since they were Jews in foreign lands, they were part of an ethnic minority that was scorned and shunned. Having accepted Christ as their Messiah, they experienced persecution as well from their own family, friends, and social environment. Some had their businesses boycotted and others were disowned by their families. This kind of pressure is not uncommon today. In seminary I had a Jewish friend whose family held a funeral for him when he accepted Christ as his Saviour.

It is into this kind of setting that James speaks about the ability of difficulty to change us. He writes:

> Consider it pure joy, my brothers, whenever you face trials of many kinds, because you know that the testing of your faith develops perseverance. Perseverance must finish its work so that you may be mature and complete, not lacking anything. If any of you lacks wisdom, he should ask God, who gives generously to all without finding fault, and it will be given to him (James 1:2-5).

James 1:4 states that trials do three things to make us usable. First, their purpose is to make us mature. Trials develop *character*. The text indicates that trials *complete* us. God *always* finishes what He starts (Phil. 1:6). God wants to completely change us. He wants to work on every portion of our being that we might be complete. Lastly, He wants us to lack nothing. This concept is used in secular Greek literature to mean fully equipped. It is used to describe an army that is equipped, capable, and victorious. God wants to make us *capable*. Pain is a process that can be used by God to accomplish this important goal.

Why does God want to change us? Isn't God satisfied with us the way we are? No. He accepts us as we are, but He is not satisfied until we are usable for Him.

A few weeks ago I went to the store to buy a new garage

door opener. I shopped, found the right one, paid for it, and took it home. It came in two boxes. I unboxed it, assembled it, hung it, and wired it. In the process, there was a lot of banging on its parts to get them to fit. A lot of tightening of its screws and bolts.

It's like that with God. He accepts us just the way we are. But He then wants to make us usable. He may need to take us out of our comfortable, neatly packaged boxes. Bang on us. Tighten here and loosen there. Whatever it takes.

If we are to be successful in pain, it is essential that God's goals become our goals. If it is our goal to be conformed to the image of His Son—to be righteous, to find our sufficiency in Him, to serve Him with the risk reduced, to be made capable and usable—then we will willingly endure whatever leads us to the goal. We will realize that the pain is worth the gain. If, however, our goal is to be happy, healthy, wealthy, and comfortable, then we will resist the trials of life and become bitter and brittle in the Master's hand. We must agree with God at the outset. Our prayer should be, "Lord, I want to be capable and usable for You. Whatever it takes, I am ready. Only go with me."

A RIGHT RESPONSE

Our willingness to cooperate with God's process of change is crucial. James gives four imperatives that create the flexibility in our spirits so that God can do His good work.

First, we are to "*consider it pure joy*" (James 1:2). This is not a command to feel happy about pain. That is unrealistic. Trouble hurts and often breaks our hearts. The word *consider* means to mentally recognize. It is a word used in accounting. Our mind is like a ledger sheet with many columns. They are labeled *terrible, get angry, get even, feel sorry for yourself, unfair, too much to bear.* On the ledger sheet of our minds, there must be a column that is headed *joy*. When trials come, we take the pencil of our faith in God and move across the sheet and place a check in the *joy* column. Why? Because we *know* that our trials will work to mature and complete us. To make us capable for use in the Master's hand. As such we can consider it pure joy! This was Christ's response, "Who for the joy set before Him, endured the cross" (Heb. 12:2).

This step transforms our attitudes. Instead of complaining and resisting, we recognize the value of our pain and as such we walk through it with our hands held high in victory.

Second, James says that this joy perspective is based on what we *know* (v. 3). We must affirm the truth that this pain is a process. A process that puts our faith to the test and then develops our perseverance which then permits God's work to come to fulfillment. Knowing that our pain is a process with a purpose gives us a reason then to hang in there and let it become complete. In this step, we must let our faith be proven. Trials will reveal the strength of our faith. Prove that your faith in God's promises, His Word, and His character is firm. Cling to Him by faith and don't let go. In so doing you will persevere.

Submit to the process (v. 4). As the *King James Version* puts it, "But let patience have her perfect work." We are all prone to pray, "Lord, take this away—and do it *now!*" If He doesn't, we chafe under it and fight against it. Perseverance must finish its work. Stay under the pressure. Let God do His work. Relent and relax. I have never known of anyone to climb off the surgery table and run all over the operating room with the doctor chasing after them, scalpel in hand. How ineffective the doctor's work would be.

When our children were small, one of them fell and cut open his eyebrow. As we walked into the emergency room, the doctor laid my son on the table, told my wife to take a seat at the end of the table, and then lectured my boy about how he had to lay perfectly still on the table. He then asked me to help hold him down.

The procedure began. I watched as he shot the anesthetic into the open wound. He then began to stitch the gash closed. I could feel it coming. I must have turned grey because the nurse escorted me into the hall and placed me in a wheelchair, put my head between my knees, and then had the audacity to ask if I wanted a popsicle! How ineffective I was. Not my son. He laid there like a little soldier. The process was completed and today his handsome face is unmarred by what would have been a big and ugly scar. It required that he submit to the process.

James then lastly directs us to pray for *wisdom* (v. 5). Many times in trouble we will feel bewildered and confused. God wants to give us His wisdom in place of our own. There is the wisdom of His Word. The wisdom that comes from knowing Him and understanding how He would respond. God gives wisdom through godly counsel. His wisdom often comes through prayer.

Left to ourselves and our earthly wisdom we will probably make matters worse. We need God's point of view in pain. As a boy I used to love to work with models. I would often impatiently start to assemble a model airplane without looking at the instructions. After all, I'd done this before. I thought I was smart enough to figure it out. Invariably, I would mess up the model. The pilot to the plane wouldn't fit into the already assembled cockpit or a wing wouldn't fasten to the fuselage—all because I had skipped a step. Is it any wonder that God counsels us to lean not on our own understanding?

We need to hear our Lord when He says that our ways are not His ways and our thoughts are not His thoughts (Isa. 55:8). He warns that there is a way that seems right unto a man, but the end thereof are the ways of death (Prov. 16:25). Seek wisdom. Assemble the broken parts of your life by His instructions.

As Proverbs 4:5-9 says, "Get wisdom, get understanding; do not forget My words or swerve from them. Do not forsake wisdom, and she will protect you; love her, and she will watch over you. Wisdom is supreme; therefore get wisdom. Though it cost all you have, get understanding. Esteem her, and she will exalt you; embrace her, and she will honor you. She will set a garland of grace on your head and present you with a crown of splendor."

Those who wish to be capable and usable will, with a spirit of joy and patience, accept God's crucible of change.

GOD'S GLORY—PART 1
Credibility and Visibility

A lot of people know where they are going and how they are going to get there. Take, for example, the materialist. He lives to accumulate. The hedonist lives for pleasure and knows right where to go to get it. The self-fulfiller lives for the big number one. Each of these has a well-defined sense of purpose.

Unfortunately, many believers either adopt the purposes of the world or have no idea what their purpose in life should be. Some have purposes that vacillate depending on who they are with or what they have recently read. Their life flows like a meandering stream. They have no voice for themselves. They are like an echo.

Thankfully, God wants to help us establish a purpose for our lives. God's purpose for us is that we *glorify* Him. It is the reason for our redemption (1 Cor. 6:19-20; Rom. 8:29). It is the all-consuming focus of our existence and the mea-

110

sure of our maturity (1 Cor. 10:31; 2 Cor. 3:18).

Basically, glorifying God means reflecting His nature. Glorifying God means we are image-bearers who mirror the love, mercy, power, righteousness, justice, and other aspects of God. It means we give visibility to His invisibility. Credibility to His existence.

God's glory is the essence of His very being. He knows that the ultimate health and welfare of the human race depends on our knowing Him. God is made known through those of us who are His children. It is our privileged assignment to reveal Him before a watching world.

God uses several means to reveal His glory. The sun, stars, and moon reveal His power and creativity. Israel revealed what God was like as He opened the sea for them and defeated armies far beyond their ability. Christ was God's glory in the flesh. The Bible reveals the glory of God. And you and I are added to the list. That puts us in significant company. It is a high and privileged responsibility. It is our purpose in living to add credibility and visibility to God.

DIFFICULTY: A PRELUDE TO GOD'S GLORY

Our children used to have an intriguing toy. It was a fireman's hat with a large red light mounted on the top. The battery-operated light would go round and round as the children walked through the house. It captured everybody's attention.

Difficulty is a lot like that. If tragedy or crisis impacts your life, people around you stop to notice. They talk to you, talk to others about you, do things to help you, and periodically ask to see how you are doing. Seemingly unnoticed, even uninteresting people draw a crowd when they go through difficulty. Trouble is often God's way of saying to the world around us, "May I have your attention, please?"

So it was with a man who had been blind from birth (John 9:1). He was well-known for his begging on the temple steps. As he begged day by day, he gained high visibility. His trouble had placed him in the limelight. If God is to be visible, then He must catch the attention and interest of a fast-moving, earthly-minded world.

Not only does the blind man capture the people's attention, but he has also *aroused their curiosity*. The disciples ask Christ, "Rabbi, who sinned, this man or his parents, that he was born blind?" (v. 2) The rabbis of Christ's day thought that consequences of the parents' sins would be reaped in the children of the sinning parents. Since this man was born blind, could it have been because of his parents? Or did he sin in his mother's womb? The curious controversy reflects the then prevalent position that the only purpose in pain was punishment for sin.

In the midst of their curiosity, Christ deepened their perspectives on pain by telling them there was another purpose. A much greater, nobler purpose.

Parenthetically, I see here in Christ a great lesson in compassion. Christ steps above the controversy with a spirit of *compassion*. He will heal the blind man's eyes. The disciples, by contrast, are more interested in the theology of the trouble than the trauma of the trouble. They are more curious than compassionate. They had seen Christ do many miracles. It would have been an act of compassion for them to have pointed out the man born blind to Christ and asked

Him to heal him. Then after the need was met, to inquire of the reason for his pain.

We are prone to the same malady. It is more comfortable to be curious about another's pain than it is to be compassionate and constructive. We often spend more time talking about people's problems than we spend reaching out to them. We spend more time wondering *why* than we do praying.

Compassion must always rise above the curiosity. Healing must always be our priority as we look toward those who hurt. It is not that we should be uninterested in truth and knowledge; it's that things need to be put in their proper place. Christ here demonstrates that God turns a compassionate face toward those who struggle. We too must look to people who hurt with a caring heart and not just a curious eye.

Christ's compassion is the beginning of the unfolding of God's purpose in this man's pain. Christ explains that the man was born blind to give *credibility* and *visibility* to God. "Neither this man nor his parents sinned . . . but this happened so that the work of God might be displayed in his life" (v. 3).

John selects this story to support the credibility of Christ's claims as God and the true Saviour of mankind (20:30-31). John consistently uses the word *work* to indicate a miracle that affirms the credibility of Christ's link to the Father and His claims as the Messiah. Christ claimed that He was sent from the Father (v. 4). This miracle would give credibility to that claim. Christ also claimed that He was the "light" of the world (v. 5). This miracle would beautifully demonstrate that claim by taking the man from darkness to light.

The man was born blind to provide visibility for God, "so that the work of God might be displayed" (v. 3). The word *displayed* literally means to reveal, to make known. God has chosen not to keep Himself a secret. Through this man's trouble, God is going to make Himself known. The invisible God will become visible. We will see the Father's compassion and power. What was only before a bit of theology would now become an experienced reality.

As Christ said, all of this would happen "in his life," that is, in the life of the man born blind. We are the channel, the stage for God's glory. Our difficulty and pain come into perspective when we see them in the light of the high privilege of giving the claims of Christ credibility and the power of God visibility.

It may be that the claim that God's "grace is sufficient" will become credible. In trouble, we can reflect God by making visible His patience and His forgiveness. We can exhibit God's willingness to suffer so that others can be helped. It may very well be that a miraculous healing will give visibility to God's power.

Recently, a woman in our church went through terribly difficult times. Her unsaved parents were overwhelmed with not only the stability that came with her confidence in Christ, but also with the tremendous outpouring of care and concern shown by her Christian friends. The trouble caught their attention as they were watching. God was glorified.

Our trouble becomes the stage of God's triumph. A stage where He can become credible and visible to a world watching with curious eyes. In this context, our pain is a prelude to fulfilling our purpose in life. Pain is a setting in which we can uniquely magnify God.

DELIGHT IN DIFFICULTY

I am struck with the unusual perspective in Paul's life in Philippians 1. He is under house arrest in Rome. He is the first century's premier apostle. Now he is incarcerated. How discouraging! The believers in Rome are opposing him, hoping to stir up trouble for him (Phil. 1:17). How defeating! At any moment Nero may pronounce the verdict of Paul's death. Surprisingly, the whole tone of Philippians 1 exudes delight.

Why?

Much of our response to difficulty centers in our expectations. When we expect comfort and get pain instead, we feel defeated. When we expect health, happiness, and prosperity, and trouble steals it from us, we then fall into the pit of disappointment and despair. Expectations determine our response to trouble.

Let's say that I come home one night and my children say, "Dad, let's go to the circus next Tuesday." To buy myself time, I may say, "Maybe—we'll see." Which, being interpreted to a child, means "yes."

I quickly forget all about it. Tuesday night I come home and they meet me at the door and say, "Dad, get ready!"

"For what?"

"For the circus!"

"Oh," I reply, "we're not going to the circus."

They then simply say, "OK, Dad, we just wanted to check," and then merrily skip off to busy themselves with some other pleasure.

I doubt it!

They will pout. Grumble. Complain. Cajole. Cry. The discouragement and depression will be deep all around us.

Because their expectations were not fulfilled.

We never outgrow that reflex reaction in pain. We shouldn't waste our time trying to adjust to broken expectations; we should adjust our expectations. There is only one expectation we should have in life and it is that Christ will be glorified in us. That He will be magnified. That through us, He will have credibility and visibility.

That was the key to Paul's response. He admits, "*I eagerly expect* and hope that I will in no way be ashamed, but will have sufficient courage so that now as always *Christ will be exalted* in my body, whether by life or by death" (Phil. 1:20). Paul's imprisonment had resulted in some being saved in Caesar's household (1:13; 4:21). Because Paul was courageous enough to be imprisoned, others became more bold to speak the Gospel (1:14). Paul's setback was only a setup for God's glory. Even in the opposition from the Roman believers, Christ was being preached (v. 18). And, if Paul should die, he would magnify the Lord in death (v. 20).

Paul's expectation, the exaltation of Christ, was fulfilled. This enabled Paul to live above defeat in the midst of devastating circumstances.

GOD'S GLORY AMONG THE MASSES

Having said this, [Jesus] spit on the ground, made some mud with the saliva, and put it on the man's eyes.

"Go," He told him, "wash in the pool of Siloam." . . . So the man went and washed, and came home seeing (John 9:6-7).

What can we expect as we glorify God through our pain? The responses of those in John 9 help us to know the kind of reception God's glory will receive around us.

First, some will see and *seek*. When his neighbors and friends saw the healed man, they couldn't believe it was the same man who had been blind. He said, "I am the man" (v. 9). Then he told them of Christ. His testimony made Christ credible and visible. They asked anxiously, "Where is this man?" (v. 12) The works of God had cut a path of pre-evangelism through the blind man's neighborhood. They sought to find Christ and know more about Him.

Why did a pagan harlot from Jericho come to believe in the God of Israel? Because God glorified Himself through Israel when He dried up the Red Sea. He demonstrated His credibility and visibility when Israel defeated the mighty armies of the Amorites. The word spread—all the way to Jericho and into Rahab's heart. God's glory through Israel cut a path of pre-evangelism in her heart (Josh. 2:8-11).

A couple in my first ministry took the time and made the effort to put their difficult marriage together on God's terms. It caught the attention of their neighbors. Seeing God glorified in their home, a couple in the neighborhood began to seek God. They came and asked why. They heard about Jesus Christ and soon received Him as Saviour.

Others will see God's works and remain *silent*. The blind man's parents were intimidated by the Pharisees. They feared they would be excommunicated from the synagogue (John 9:18-22). Many fear the price of claiming Christ as Saviour. What will He demand? What will they lose in gaining Him? So they silently watch. They take notes in their hearts. That's good. God will work quietly in their silence to capitalize on what they have seen.

Then there are those who will be *set against* what they see. No one knew more about this event than the Pharisees. They interviewed the blind man twice (vv. 13-16, 24-34) and his parents once (vv. 18-23). Yet the Pharisees refused to accept the clear evidence. Some are so set against God that they refuse to seek Him regardless of the evidence. Think of what they did to Christ who was a walking catalog of evidence. In the face of the dramatic display of God's credibility and visibility through Christ, they crucified Him. We should never assume that all people will come to Christ when they see Him magnified in our trouble.

OBEDIENT WITNESS

One key question remains. If God should choose my life and my pain as a platform for His glory, how can I cooperate? How can I be sure that His purpose will come to pass?

Two things in the blind man's response are key to his privileged place in God's plan. First, in his trouble he *obeyed the Master* (John 9:6-7). Christ put mud on his eyes and told him to wash in the pool of Siloam. "So the man went and washed, and came home seeing" (v. 7). The revelation of God's glory depended on the man's obedience to Christ's commands. So it is with us. Our unconditional surrender to all that Christ tells us to do sets the stage for His glory.

If my pain is from the injury of another's careless actions against me, then I hear Christ say, "Forgive them." That's the pool in which I wash my eyes. When money fails, I hear Christ say, "Seek ye first the kingdom of God, and His righteousness; and all these things shall be added unto you"

(Matt. 6:33, KJV). Therefore, I don't forsake my stewardship to His kingdom; I don't abandon righteousness to make a little extra money. I don't forsake my family responsibilities. I stay in the path of righteousness so that God may do something special to glorify Himself. I refuse to become bitter. I trust God to deal with my enemies and I love them in return. I refuse anger. I refuse to stop reaching out with a servant's heart. I wash in the pool of His will. I obey.

The second key to cooperating with God's plan is to give *witness*. The blind man happily gave credit to Christ before his neighbors, his parents, and the hostile Jewish leaders. He did it with tact and with courage. He did it even when it meant dismissal from the temple (John 9:34).

As God works in your life, tactfully proclaim His glory. Give credit where credit is due. If God delivers you through prayer, then let it be known that your God answers prayer. If God provides sustaining grace, then let it be known that you are making it because His mighty hand is supporting you. Christ opened the blind man's eyes to bring glory to His Father. Nobody in your world will know the credibility and visibility of God if you lock them up as hidden secrets in the closet of your life!

When the psalmist asked God to help him, he prayed, "May God be gracious to us and bless us and make His face shine upon us" (Ps. 67:1).

Why? That God's ways may "be known on earth, and Your salvation among all nations" (v. 2).

If God heals you, helps you, holds you, or delivers you, let your whole world know.

Their wedding was scheduled for August. Several months before, cancer was discovered in one lung of the bride-to-be.

They postponed and she began her treatments. Many prayed—specifically and intensely. After her first treatment, the doctors were amazed. They could find no trace of the cancer.

At Christmas, the bride and groom were united in marriage. They made it clear to me that they wanted all at the wedding to know what God had done. It was my joy.

A woman in our church came to me and said, "Pastor, I have a confession to make." Though unaccustomed as I am to taking confessions, I listened. She told me how several weeks earlier, her husband had written a check for God's work through their local church. This couple's business had been slow and they were financially to the wall. She told him they couldn't afford to do it. He replied, "We can't afford *not* to do it." So they did. She said that since they took that step of obedience, God has blessed them beyond their dreams. Their business increased fourfold. "I learned a great lesson, Pastor, about the faithfulness of God. I wish I could tell everyone. In fact," she continued, "you have my permission to tell anyone you wish."

We have a purpose, a divine destiny. Our purpose is to glorify God through our lives. If God should select you to bring glory to Him in this world through pain, do it well. Obey. Bear witness. Through your suffering, some may seek and find the Saviour. Let them hear you sing:

> To God be the glory,
> Great things He hath done!

GOD'S GLORY—PART II
Job's Unusual Task

Why?

Why me? Why now? Why again? Why don't You help me? Why God, why?

Trouble persistently taunts us with its questions. Yet God does supply us with answers. He teaches us that pain exists because of the problem of sin. We know that pain can be used to conform us to Christ's image, that pain from righteousness pays off in power. It is pain that draws us from disobedience to obedience. We may experience the painful tearing away of the layers of our sufficiency to help us become God sufficient. God may permit pain to reduce the risk in our lives. God may even use pain to make us usable for Him or to demonstrate His power and glory on the earth.

But what do you do when all the answers to pain elude you? When you shout *Why* and there is a great silence. When

121

from your perspective, the suffering makes absolutely no sense at all.

So it was for Job. Job suffered intensely over a long period of time. Though Job never knew why, there was a reason for his pain. With God, there *always* is a reason. He never permits pain without a purpose. We have the distinct advantage of knowing that purpose.

JOB'S SUFFERING WAS A SHOWCASE

> Job was blameless and upright; he feared God and shunned evil. He had seven sons and three daughters, and he owned 7,000 sheep, 3,000 camels, 500 yoke of oxen and 500 donkeys, and had a large number of servants. He was the greatest man among all the people of the East (Job. 1:1-3).

The stage is set in the verses that follow this description of Job (vv. 6-12).

In essence, Satan says to God, "Job is righteous and worships You because You are good to him. You have made him rich and You have not permitted any evil to befall him. If You took all this away, he would curse You to Your face."

Can you grasp what Satan has just said? He has said that God is not worthy of a man's worship and loyalty in and of Himself. Instead, God has to buy our love. Men do not value God for who He is, but only for what He does for them. The glory of God has been slandered in front of the heavenly host. It's as though all the eyes of the universe turn questioningly toward God. Is God worthy of a man's worship and praise regardless? What kind of God is He anyway?

We go to great lengths to protect our reputations from slander. By comparison, our reputations aren't worth being concerned about. General Ariel Sharon traveled to New York to file a $50 million lawsuit against *Time* magazine who had accused him of complicity in a massacre in Beirut, Lebanon. He had to clear his name. General William West-moreland took CBS to court in a multimillion dollar lawsuit to protect himself against their supposed slandering of his reputation. How much more should God's name be upheld. God could not simply ignore Satan's charge; it was far too serious.

Who would come to God's defense? Job. Job is called upon to prove a point on God's behalf. He will suffer to prove the worthiness of God. There could be no higher calling. God, as the sentinel at the gate of Job's life, opens the gate and Job's troubles begin at the hand of Satan.

Ancient Chinese theater had a peculiar approach to their plays. They would construct the stage on two levels. On the lower level, the play would progress as written. On the upper level, the conclusion of the play was acted out. Since the audience knew the final act, they would often shout words of encouragement to the hero when the villain was about to overcome him. They would call for him to "hang in there"—because they knew that all would turn out well in the end.

I feel that way with Job. I feel like shouting, "Job, don't flinch. Make it through. You can't imagine how important this is." I cheer as Job finishes the first act in this tragic drama. He has lost everything, including his sons and daughters (Job 1:13-19). Yet, he closes Act I in grief and agony, still worshiping his God. "At this, Job got up and tore his robe and shaved his head. Then he fell to the ground in worship and said: 'Naked I came from my mother's womb, and naked I will depart. The Lord gave and the Lord has taken away; may the name of the Lord be praised.' In all this, Job did not sin by charging God with wrongdoing" (vv. 20-22). Job proved the worthiness of God to be praised regardless.

Satan is persistent. He slanders God again by saying that the problem is that God had not permitted him to touch Job's body (2:1-5). Satan assumes that Job will fold and curse God if his health and comfort are at stake. Satan will stop at nothing. He is willing to waste anything and anybody to get to God's glory. God trusts Job with the challenge and prohibits Satan from taking Job's life.

> So Satan went out from the presence of the Lord and afflicted Job with painful sores from the soles of his feet to the top of his head. Then Job took a piece of broken pottery and scraped himself with it as he sat among the ashes (vv. 7-8).

Job's wife enters the scene at this point and comforts Job with some sage advice: "Curse God and die!" (v. 9) That's just what Satan wanted Job to do. That would play right into his hand. My spirit shouts to Job as he plays out the scene on the first level. "Don't do it, Job. Don't give up."

Job speaks. In the midst of the ashes, he affirms, " 'You are talking like a foolish woman. Shall we accept good from God, and not trouble?' In all this, Job did not sin in what he said" (v. 10).

Job has done it. God's name has been magnified in the midst of his misery. And all the time, Job had no way of knowing why. Yet Job was loyal to God above his possessions and beyond his personal comfort. God is indeed a worthy God.

On the stage of our own lives Satan reduplicates the scene. God's Word calls him the "accuser of our brothers, who accuses them before our God day and night" (Rev. 12:10). It's as though he stands and says:

- Look at him. He professes You as Lord, yet he values his pornography more than You.
- Her affair is worth more than You are to her.
- They curse You for their pain.
- They don't love You for who You are. Comfort, health, and happiness are all more valuable to them.

It is a high calling to prove the worthiness of God in the face of Satan's accusations. Whether in pain or pleasure, we can constantly prove with our lives that God is worthy above all else in life. That was Job's privilege. Even though he had done it in the face of intense trouble.

There were some other reasons for Job's suffering. God knew that we needed a demonstration that true faith in God is more than a self-serving faith. I hear it all the time. Some people say that our faith is only a crutch, a means whereby we can keep our lives together, a means to get blessed now and then. Satan kicked the crutches out from under Job and Job proved that his faith was anchored in God.

Some religionists will tell you that if you have enough

faith, you can be happy, healthy, and wealthy. Faith to them is a way to *get* good things from God. Job lost it all. Yet he remained a man of faith.

Faith is our unshakable belief in God, His Word, and His character. True faith stands above and beyond the trouble and triumphs of life. When life demolished Job, it did not demolish his faith. If trouble demolishes our faith, it is a reflection that our faith was only a faith for protection, peace, and pleasure. A shallow, selfish faith.

Job's suffering also proves that some of our trouble may be the result of an invisible conflict taking place in the spiritual realm. Struggles that have meaning beyond my job, my roommate, my family, or my peace. Ephesians 6 clearly speaks to the issue of a whole network of Satan's forces battling against God and against His people. Paul writes, "For our struggle is not against flesh and blood, but against the rulers, against the authorities, against the powers of this dark world and against the spiritual forces of evil in the heavenly realms" (Eph. 6:12).

It is important for us to know that some of the "whys" in our lives are answered in a higher realm. Sometimes we struggle with pain to prove ultimate universal principles before the throne of God. Not all of suffering has an answer on earth but sometimes is part of a conflict in another sphere. A sphere in which our faithfulness generates a victory on behalf of God.

Lastly, Job's suffering helps to chart a course for us. Job shows us a way to suffer well. He is a model and an example. He demonstrates that you don't need to have all your questions answered to survive. Job had *no* answers. He had no idea of what was happening beyond the reaches of this earth. All he had was God and a faith that refused to quit. A belief that in spite of all that was happening around him, he trusted that God was still God and as such deserved his unflinching allegiance. Job charted the course through the waters of seemingly senseless trouble.

As a pacesetter for us, Job demonstrates success in suffering in two ways. First, we can all identify with him in that he suffered severely. Second, Job made it through this severe struggle because he knew God.

JOB SUFFERED SEVERELY

When we hurt we are often encouraged to turn to Christ who suffered for us, leaving an example for us to follow. And well we should. But we are tempted to think that He had a divine edge. Job was *only* human. That doesn't discount Christ's help in our need; it simply provides Job as an example of a mortal who made it. Notice the breadth of Job's suffering.

Job suffered the loss of all his *external worth*—children, houses, livestock, riches. Even Job's wife was disgusted with him. He lost it *all*. His world became a heap of ashes. Many of us base our worth and self-esteem on externals. We shouldn't, but we often do. It's where we live, what we drive, who we know, the size of our bank account, or the title on the door of our corporate office that establishes our worth and sense of self-esteem. But God calls us to base our esteem and worth in our relationship with Him. As we internalize our relationship with God, we develop true self-esteem and true worth. That's where Job was. Even though Job was one of the most righteous and richest men of his day, when everything was demolished around him, *he* was not demolished. He still had his God and his God had him.

Job's suffering was also *physical, mental, and emotional* (2:2). His body began to disintegrate; he was racked with pain. Job went through great seasons of depression and mental confusion which were complicated by his so-called friends.

Job was subjected to the *bad counsel of good friends.* It began with Job's wife. Let's not be too hard on her. Have you ever watched a loved one suffer? You know how quickly it gets to you. In despair, she counseled him, "Curse God and die!" (2:9) Yet Job found the strength to resist the temptations of his wife's words.

Then there were three friends who came and gave advice: "Job, you have sinned. That's why this happened to you. Repent and recover."

Nine times they repeat their charge. Nine times Job says, "It's not true." Back and forth they go, wearing one another down.

Even well-meaning friends tend to complicate our trouble. They mean their words to be like salve, but instead they are like swords. These friends are like those modern-day prophets who tell us that *all* trouble, sickness, and sorrow come from unconfessed sin in our lives. May God shield us from this kind of destructive advice. It was not true of Job. He suffered for a more noble cause. What he needed from his friends was *grace,* not guilt. At the end of Job's suffering, God calls the three friends before Him and reproves them for their bad counsel and calls on them to repent (42:7-9).

Job's suffering was severe because of the *memories* (29:2-25). When we lose, we are left only with the memories.

Difficulty often leaves us without the things we used to possess. Without people who were precious to us. Without a husband. Without a wife. Without good health. Without fame. Without income. Then the memories of all that used to be haunt our spirits. The memories of what we had and lost. They are memories that only serve to magnify our misery.

Job's suffering was also severe because he had *no support*. Who was his psychiatrist? Where was his pastor? What medication could he take? Job had no books to read on grief and pain. He didn't even have a "significant loss seminar" that he could attend. No family. Friends were a problem. He couldn't even read the Bible. Yet Job made it. He and God alone.

In all of this, Satan has reduced Job to the irreducible minimum—Job and his God. That's right where Satan wants him. Now Job, all you have is God. Will you curse Him or praise His name?

Job is indeed a pacesetter. Under *severe difficulty* he refuses to depart from loyally worshiping his God. And in all of it, he didn't know why. How did he do it?

JOB KNEW HIS GOD

The theme of the Book of Job is not patience, though we learn something of patience from Job's life (James 5:10-11). The theme is not Job and Satan. It is not even Satan and God. The theme of this book is not suffering.

The theme of the Book of Job is God. Who is God? And is He worthy of man's unconditional, uncompromised allegiance? Does God have the right to exercise His sovereignty?

These are the issues of the book. Does God have the right to call the shots in our lives even when we don't understand? When it makes no sense, Job answers, "Yes!" *YES!* A thousand times, yes. Yes, in spite of everything.

What did Job know about God that enabled him in trouble?

Job knew that God had the right to be *sovereign in life* (Job 1:21). God permitted Job's life to turn upside down. "The Lord gave, and the Lord hath taken away; blessed be the name of the Lord" (v. 21, KJV). We don't love God for what He does for us in life; we love Him because He is the God of our life. The day after Christ fed the 5,000, the same people showed up the next day for another spectacular meal. Christ refused. Many left Him that day. They were in it for the "goodies." When Christ told His followers that they would be persecuted for His sake, Scripture says that many left Him (John 6:53-66).

On the poverty-stricken island of Haiti, children follow you down the street begging for money. If you give them some, they keep following you. If you refuse, they scorn you and walk away. How tragic that some of us treat God that way.

God is the sovereign over all of life. A friend of mine officiated at the burial of a little baby. As the mourners walked up the hillside to the gravesite, the minister admitted that he really didn't know what to say. The mother of the child, with tears on her cheeks, said quietly, "The Lord gives and the Lord takes away. Blessed be the name of the Lord."

Job also knew that God was *sovereign in death*. In the face of death, Job said, "Though He slay me, yet will I hope in Him" (Job 13:15). It is as though Job says, "Lord, even if

You take my life, I will still affirm my trust in You. Nothing, not even death will sever my loyal allegiance to Your name" (see Phil. 1:20-21).

Job knew that God was *sovereign in wisdom and in power*. Near the end of his testing, Job teeters in his confusion and pain. God meets him and stabilizes his failing heart by reminding Job of His infinite, unchallenged wisdom and power (chaps. 38—41). God asks, "Were you there when I created the heavens and the earth? Did you ever see their cornerstone? Where are their foundations laid?" On and on, question after question. God is driving home His point. He is so vastly superior to us in wisdom and power that anything less than submission to His plan for our lives would be foolish. In all that God does, though it may be painful, though it may escape our understanding, yet He is wise. Always wise.

Affirming God's sovereignty in life, death, wisdom, and power, Job was able to say, "God, I trust You." That's how Job made it. And through it all, he proved the point. He shamed Satan and glorified the matchless name of God.

I love him for it.

He is my hero.

Job realized that in suffering the issue is not *why*. The issue is *who!* That too is the issue for us. We rest in the reality that our God is the true and the living God, worthy of our trust regardless. We affirm that He has the right to be the sovereign God of our life, death, wisdom, and power. Though this may not make the hurt any less painful, it *does* get us through victoriously in a way that honors Him.

Since God always knows what He is doing, all we have to know is Him. When the whys swarm around us, when our question marks go unanswered, when all the answers seem so shallow—get beyond them to the who. You can trust God. He'll see you through.

> Oh, the depth of the riches of the wisdom and knowledge of God! How unsearchable His judgments, and His paths beyond tracing out! Who has known the mind of the Lord? Or who has been His counselor? Who has ever given to God, that God should repay him? For from Him and through Him and to Him are all things. To Him be the glory forever! Amen (Rom. 11:33-36).

PROSPERITY
Why Do the Wicked Prosper?

Why do the righteous suffer?

Though this question often plagues our minds, we should not be surprised when the righteous suffer. It conforms us to the image of Christ. It gives us power in witness. It instills the valuable strength of God-sufficiency and reduces the risk in our ministry for God. It refines us to make us capable and usable. It catches the attention of a watching world so that God's glory may be seen as He becomes credible and visible through our suffering. It may even be used in a sphere far beyond ourselves to glorify God in the universe.

Don't pity the righteous who suffer. They have a divine edge. Their resource in pain is the reality that God is there and they only experience what He permits. And, all that He permits is guaranteed by the kind of God He is. The righteous suffer with the knowledge that Christ has conquered. Christ gives both grace and glory in the midst of pain.

The question that plagues me is not so much why do the righteous suffer, but why do the wicked prosper?

Why is it that my competitor in business can cheat his customers and strike unethical deals and drive a new Cadillac, while in my commitment to righteousness I have to drive a beat-up old car? Why does my neighbor, who goes fishing every Sunday morning while I'm at church, catch the biggest and best fish when I can hardly catch a thing on Monday? Why are the ungodly those who belong to the jet set? Why should my neighbor, who has been cheating on his wife for years, have such nice children while mine are driving me crazy? Why is it so hard and challenging to walk the Christian walk when unsaved people seem to have no restraints at all?

INSTABILITY

The psalmist struggled with this as well. In fact, it created a tremendous instability and vulnerability in his life. "As for me, my feet had almost slipped; I had nearly lost my foothold. For I envied the arrogant when I saw the prosperity of the wicked" (Ps. 73:2-3).

Envying the wicked puts us in a precarious place. It is dangerous to our spiritual health. Think of how many of God's people have compromised themselves to try to keep up with the pagan world. It is a great temptation to worship at the temple of prosperity. It is easy to begin to suspect that righteousness is less than rewarding, a divine deterrent to wealth and gain.

If all we see is the world around us, then we will surely fall. The psalmist looked around him and felt absolutely cheated when he compared his life to the prosperity of the pagans. In his misery, he relates every detail of their gain. People who are in the clutches of misery always can give detailed accounts of their problems. Over and over again we rehearse our reasons for feeling so bad. In the process, our problems often become somewhat exaggerated. So it was with Asaph, the author of Psalm 73.

> For I envied the arrogant when I saw the prosperity of the wicked. They have no struggles; their bodies are healthy and strong. They are free from the burdens common to man; they are not plagued by human ills. Therefore pride is their necklace; they clothe themselves with violence. From their callous hearts comes iniquity; the evil conceits of their minds know no limits. They scoff, and speak with malice; in their arrogance they threaten oppression. Their mouths lay claim to heaven, and their tongues take possessions of the earth. Therefore their people turn to them and drink up waters in abundance. They say, "How can God know? Does the Most High have knowledge?"
> This is what the wicked are like—always carefree, they increase in wealth (Ps. 73:3-12).

SELF-PITY

At this point, Asaph throws himself a pity party. In his pity, he bemoans the fact that his commitment to personal purity has netted him nothing (Ps. 73:13). A slight exaggeration— but when you are into self-pity, it's hard to be positive.

Surely in vain have I kept my heart pure; in vain
have I washed my hands in innocence. All day
long I have been plagued; I have been punished
every morning. If I had said, "I will speak thus," I
would have betrayed this generation of Your children. When I tried to understand all this, it was
oppressive to me (Ps. 73:13-16).

Asaph is obviously more interested in cash than in character. He wants his righteousness to pay off in dollars and
cents, in physical strength rather than in spiritual health. He
wants his God to function like a heavenly Santa Claus. And
since He hasn't, Asaph is discouraged and ready to drop out.
He is walking around defeated, pretending that everything is
OK (v. 15).

Had I been alive in Naboth's day I would have struggled
with the issue of pagan prosperity. Naboth was a common
Israelite who owned a portion of land on which he had
planted a vineyard. King Ahab wanted Naboth's land for an
herb garden. He invited Naboth to talk with him and Naboth refused. That was his family's land. It was Naboth's
heritage. In that day, inherited land was a family treasure to
be passed on for generations. No price could buy it from
Naboth. Naboth was a man of true values.

Ahab, the unjust king of Israel, pouted in his bedroom.
Jezebel, his wife, asked him what was wrong. He shared
how he couldn't have the land for his herb garden. How sad!

Well, Jezebel would see to it that Ahab got his garden. She
hired two false witnesses who testified that Naboth had
cursed God and the king. They took Naboth outside the city
and stoned him to death. Ahab had his herb garden (1 Kings

21:1-16).

Though God ultimately dealt with Ahab and Jezebel, at this point my heart cries out, "Where is God? Why do the wicked prosper?"

GOD'S BIG PICTURE

In the scope of eternity, the wicked do not prosper. Just in the knick of time, Asaph looked to God for his answer. "It was oppressive to me till I entered the sanctuary of God; then I understood *their final destiny*" (Ps. 73:16-17).

Destiny. Life is far more than the here and now. Life spans the years on into eternity. When the psalmist looked to God, his perspective changed drastically. He ceased envying the wicked and found spiritual stability again.

I have a friend who says that if all you see is the here and now, you will misunderstand everything. How true. We must reject the two-dimensional focus of the here and now and let the third dimension of God's perspective always be a part of our perceptions.

As a child, I enjoyed "3-D" comic books. A special set of cardboard glasses came with the comic books. Without the glasses, the books were blurred and unclear. With the glasses, they became distinct and alive with action and color. Seeing life through God's glasses will always clarify and provide an accurate assessment of life around us.

From God's point of view, the wicked are not in an enviable position. As the psalmist says, "Surely You place them on slippery ground; You cast them down to ruin. How suddenly are they destroyed, completely swept away by terrors! As a dream when one awakes, so when You arise, O

Lord, You will despise them as fantasies" (Ps. 73:18-20).

Is it a sign of prosperity to stand before God and hear Him say, "Depart from Me, you who are cursed, into the eternal fire prepared for the devil and his angels" (Matt. 25:41). As Christ said, "What good will it be for a man if he gains the whole world, yet forfeits his soul?" (16:26)

In Luke 12 Christ told of a wealthy man who was so prosperous that he had to tear down his old barns and build new ones. He said to himself, " 'You have plenty of good things laid up for many years. Take life easy; eat, drink and be merry.' But God said to him, 'You fool! This very night your life will be demanded from you. Then who will get what you have prepared for yourself ?' " (Luke 12:19-20) Christ concluded by saying, "This is how it will be with anyone who stores up things for himself but is not rich toward God" (Luke 12:21).

SAND CASTLES

Our family often vacations in Florida. We love the sand and the ocean. When we arrive, my plans are to hit the beach and relax. My children's plans are to play in the water and build sand castles. They usually succeed in dragging me to the water's edge where plans for a phenomenal sand castle are begun. I reluctantly begin to help (strictly parental duty), but soon find myself excitedly absorbed in the project. In fact, about halfway through, the kids are off somewhere else as I am designing and building the most spectacular sand castle on the beach. Seaweed forms ivy on the walls. Towers are topped with flags. Weeds from the dunes make palm trees for the landscape. People stop and inquire. Some say, "Who built that?" I nod proudly. Then it's time to go home. I leave the labor of my hands, the product of my own creativity. The next day we return. My sand castle is gone, washed out to sea. The tide has done me in.

So it is with the fleeting nature of earthly prosperity in the tide of God's judgment. What good is it if you have one big inning yet lose the whole game? From God's point of view, the wicked are not in an enviable position.

Yet why should they prosper even now? I am convinced it is designed as living proof of God's mercy and grace. What a picture of God's willingness to withhold judgment and give us what we don't deserve. The prosperity of the wicked is a divine reminder of God's mercy and grace. As we see the wicked prosper, our own hearts should overflow with praise because we too are recipients of that mercy and grace.

Not only is the prosperity of the wicked proof of God's mercy and grace, but it is also proof of the perversity of human hearts. God's overflowing goodness drives men to greater independence, rebellion, and wickedness. The prosperity of the wicked will quiet the objection of some who will want to excuse themselves from judgment by saying, "If You had been good to me, if You had made me prosperous, I would have believed in You!" Not so. Mankind's heart is "deceitful above all things" (Jer. 17:9).

TRUE PROSPERITY

Asaph comes before God embarrassed for envying the wicked. He admits to his shame. "I was senseless and ignorant; I was a brute beast before You" (Ps. 73:22).

Then Asaph redefines prosperity. He affirms that in God

he has true prosperity. That is why he begins the psalm with the joyful acclamation, "Surely God is good to Israel, to those who are pure in heart" (v. 1).

Asaph is prosperous because of God's continued presence with him (v. 23). As the writer of Hebrews says, "Keep your lives free from the love of money and be content with what you have, because God has said, 'Never will I leave you; never will I forsake you' " (Heb. 13:5). If God is with us, we have all we will ever need.

Asaph prospers because of God's protection. "You hold me by my right hand" (Ps. 73:23). He prospers in the fact that God guides him (v. 24). Those apart from God do not have the prosperity of His guidance. The best they can do is experiment in the darkness. Ultimately, God's people prosper in the ultimate reward of their faith. "Afterward You will take me into glory" (v. 24). It is the certain reality of heaven. The arrival of the time when God will wipe away every tear from our eyes. When there will be no more death or mourning, crying, or pain. When the old order passes away and we hear Him say, "I am making everything new!" (Rev. 21:4-5)

Don Wyrtzen has captured the strength of the coming prosperity of heaven in his song, *Finally Home.*

> When engulfed by the terror of
>   tempestuous sea,
> Unknown waves before you roll;
> At the end of doubt and peril is
>   eternity,
> Though fear and conflict seize
>   your soul:

When surrounded by the blackness of
   the darkest night,
O how lonely death can be;
At the end of this long tunnel is a
   shining light,
For death is swallowed up in victory!
But just think of stepping on shore
   and finding it heaven!
Of touching a hand and finding it God's!
Of breathing new air and finding it
   celestial!
Of waking up in glory and finding it
   home!

The psalmist concludes his discourse on true prosperity by
rejoicing in his God.

Whom have I in heaven but You? And being with
You, I desire nothing on earth. My flesh and my
heart may fail, but God is the strength of my heart
and my portion forever. Those who are far from
You will perish; You will destroy all who are
unfaithful to You. But as for me, it is good to be
near God. I have made the Sovereign Lord my
refuge; I will tell of all Your deeds (Psalm 73:25-
28).

True prosperity is found in God's in-depth, long-range
goodness to His people.

PERSEVERANCE
Keep On Keeping On

The bumper sticker read, "When the going gets tough the tough go shopping!"

It is tough to hang in there when things are tough. Shopping would be a nice alternative. Nevertheless, one of the frustrating things about pain is that it's impossible to walk away from it. You must stay in the ring and seek to survive, seek to conquer, seek to win. That requires stick-to-itiveness. And sticking to it requires perseverance.

I left seminary several years ago with an unflinching commitment to the doctrine of the perseverance of the saints. I soon discovered that on a practical level, the saints don't persevere all that well. As a young pastor, I noted that God's flock was often more committed to comfort than to character, to convenience more than to commitment, to cash more than to Christ. It was a unique brand of disposable discipleship. A Christianity that was good in pleasure, but not good in pain—so I hammered away in the pulpit, trying to call God's people to perseverance.

In time, I encountered a few difficulties. Now, to my surprise, I didn't persevere all that well myself. I found that when the going got tough, I was prone to wander—spiritually, mentally, and emotionally.

We need a fresh call for the stick-to-itiveness of the saints. Saints who refuse to curse God in pain. Who refuse bitterness. Who refuse to "go it alone." Who refuse to buy the recommendations and remedies of the world. Who claim righteousness as their ultimate cause in every situation. Who say with Job, "The Lord gave and the Lord has taken away; may the name of the Lord be praised" (Job 1:21). Who affirm Job's faith personally. The faith that claims, "Though He slay me, yet will I hope in Him" (Job 13:15). Who kneel with Christ in their Garden of Gethsemane and pray as He prayed that the cup be removed, and yet with a unique yieldedness surrender their will to the will of the Father. Who find that God's grace is sufficient. Who go for the grace and reach for the glory.

PERSEVERANCE IS THE KEY

Keeping on in a crisis requires that we have the steady and solid foundation of perseverance. The author of Hebrews exhorts his readers who were under severe pressure, "Since we are surrounded by such a great cloud of witnesses, let us throw off everything that hinders and the sin that so easily entangles, and let us run with perseverance the race marked out for us" (Heb. 12:1). The race marked out for them was an obstacle course. It required that they face the obstacles of rejection, loss of friends, economic difficulty, and daily persecution. Perseverance would be their indispensable companion in trouble.

I have friends who are runners. They have kindled my interest in marathons, those massive, grueling 26-mile runs. As I have watched some of the races, I note that the runners have friends along the way who throw them towels or hand them cups of something to drink. I sense that these companions are essential to the runners' success. It's like that with perseverance. You can't run the course of trouble without it.

What does it mean to persevere? In the original text, *perseverance* was literally made up of two words. One meaning "to remain." The other word meaning "under." This is the essence of perseverance. It is the ability to stay under the pressure of our difficulty with a good spirit. We usually want to squirt out from under the pressure. To be done. To hurry the sunshine. If you have ever placed your thumb on a wet watermelon seed and applied pressure, you know that it immediately squirts out from under your thumb. God intended that watermelon seeds would do well under pressure. They were to be pressed into the ground. Swollen in the rain-soaked earth. Baked in the summer heat of the sun. Then at just the right time they are to send a fresh green shoot through the parched earth, to blossom and bear the kind of fruit that blesses many.

God intends that we, too, will blossom under pressure. Perseverance gives God the time to do His work of blossoming through us. That's why James exhorts us to submit to the trial and let perseverance "finish its work" (James 1:4). Refusing to persevere aborts the work of God that is being conceived in us.

Pressure comes in many different forms. For you, it may be the pressure of continued physical pain. Emotional distress. The breaking up of a valued relationship. Rejection by your peers. A wayward child. A struggle with temptation. A haunting from your past. The pull of priorities. Overwhelming responsibilities. Economic stress. Demolished dreams. It may be, as Paul writes, that you are pressed on every side (2 Cor. 4:8).

There is an ancient torture called being drawn and quartered. In this torture, a horse is tied to each ankle and each wrist of the victim. Then the horses are marched slowly, each in a different direction. There are times that pressures and problems seem to be ripping us apart. Times when we will feel drawn and quartered.

But in it all, there is one constant reality that keeps our heads above the flood—and that is perseverance. The ability to stay under the pressure until the pain has resulted in God's gain. How is perseverance developed? What is at the core?

THE STRENGTH OF PERSEVERANCE

Hebrews 11 provides a roster of saints who persevered under phenomenal pressure. It is a listing of some of those who metaphorically comprise the great "cloud of witnesses" that now surround us.

We read that they

> were tortured and refused to be released, so that they might gain a better resurrection. Some faced jeers and flogging, while still others were chained and put in prison. They were stoned; they were

sawed in two; they were put to death by the
sword. They went about in sheepskins and goat
skins, destitute, persecuted and mistreated—the
world was not worthy of them. They wandered in
deserts and mountains, and in caves and holes in
the ground (Heb. 11:35-38).

Somehow their real life experiences help put my problems
into perspective. Not that mine hurt any less, but in these
lives I get a glimpse of true perseverance.

Note the commentary on their lives: "These were all
commended for their faith" (v. 39). They persevered. They
got a good report. A "well done, thou good and faithful
servant" (Matt. 25:21, KJV). What was at the center of their
commendation? Their *faith*. It was the very essence, the
strength of their perseverance.

Have faith, brother! is the exhortation of Hebrews 11. Faith
always has an object, something it attaches itself to. Our
faith is only as good as the source to which it clings. You can
nail, glue, bolt, reinforce, and permanently fasten a support
beam to a wall. But if the wall falls down, the support beam
is no good.

God is our solid, unshakeable, sure wall in trouble. No
weight can pull Him down. Faith means grabbing hold of
His character and believing that He is good, all-powerful,
caring, forgiving, tender, and just. True faith refuses to let
go of those realities. Faith means taking God's promises,
claiming them, and clinging to them. It is grasping His
Word and applying it to our pain. While faith does not
always give us answers, it does always keep us steady and
secure. It focuses our hearts and minds on the light at the end

of the tunnel, the light of God's glory revealed in us.

As I review this tremendous cast of suffering saints, I ask myself, *In what did they place their faith?* I note a common thread. They suffered as a part of God's *plan*. They believed He had a *purpose* for their lives. He had promised them a plan, and though it didn't materialize until after they went to be with Him (Heb. 11:39), they affirmed it in their lives and refused to bail out.

Martie and I feel strongly about teaching our children to swim. When our eldest son was old enough to begin his lessons, we signed him up at the local YWCA. Martie packed his bag and off he and I went. We went into the locker room where I helped him get dressed. I could almost see the Olympic medal around his neck. I sent him out to the pool and made my way to the room where the parents watched the lessons. The room was separated from the pool by a large glass wall. I watched as my son took one look at the water, backed up against the wall, and began to cry his little eyes out.

The swimming instructor looked toward the parents' room as if to say, "Who's responsible for him?"

I raised my hand and she sent Joe back to the dressing room. I met him there. He came in sobbing, refusing to learn to swim. I coaxed him and warned him—all to no avail. Then I told him that there was a purpose to learning how to swim. Maybe he'd be fishing some day with his own little boy who would fall into the lake. Who would rescue him?

Well, that seemed to help a little bit, so I told him I would come to as many lessons as possible. We made an agreement. Anytime he became afraid, he would look to the parents' room and I would give him a signal—the "OK" sign. It would remind him that his father had a purpose for the swimming lessons.

The lessons proceeded well; the signal was working. Then the day came when the children were to duck their heads under water. This was a monumental difficulty in my little son's life. The children lined up and one by one placed their faces in the water. It was Joe's turn. He looked at me with a sense of anxiety. I flashed the signal and under he went. He came up with a big smile and a sense of victory. He had done it!

What got him through? When he was ready to fold, he looked to his father.

It's the same kind of faith that strengthens our resolve to persevere. We look to the Father and remember that though our problems may be difficult and threatening, our Father's plan and purpose are worth the effort. Hence, we keep on.

MOTIVATION TO PERSEVERE

The Old Testament saints suffered without seeing the promise of the Messiah fulfilled. They went through their deep waters with only a "hope so" faith. They were willing to do their part for what was yet to come. But "God had planned something better for us so that only together with us would they be made perfect" (Heb. 11:40).

We have a "know so" faith. Christ has come. All that the Old Testament saints suffered to conceive has been born through our Saviour. He has conquered sin, death, hell, suffering, and sorrow. We are on the victory side. We do our part for Him in pain or pleasure, blessing and buffeting, with the *confidence* of His victory.

Not only do we have a better way, but we also play a part in completing what the Old Testament saints have begun. As the plan of God stretches from age to age, some saints in years gone by invest their lives to make possible that which is to come. Those who follow complete that which others have begun. In the scope of biblical history, we are very much like the last runner in a relay race. Throughout the Old Testament, many people suffered to preserve and produce the Messiah seed. Christ suffered to conquer sin and death and to provide the message of eternal life. The apostles and the first-century church suffered greatly to plant God's church.

Now it's our turn. We take our places. We are completers. We perfect what they have begun. In a very real sense, when we refuse to persevere, when we refuse to do our part in God's plan and purpose, we abort what they suffered to conceive.

I am motivated when I think that I am not in this alone. Like a runner in the last lap of a relay race, I am motivated to successfully complete what those who went before worked so hard to begin. I am a part of God's grand big picture. I will do my part. I too will be faithful in good times and bad. I want God to count on me!

MY TURN

Hebrews 12:1 ushers me into a great Roman arena. The Holy Spirit hands me the baton and now I must run the race marked for me. I notice that the track is an obstacle course, full of the pitfalls of the world system. I see more buffetings than blessings on the track ahead of me and I say, "I can't do it! Not me, Lord."

As I begin to hand the baton back, I see the great crowd that fills the arena. They all have run before and persevered. They all have finished triumphantly by faith. They did their part in their day.

I see Abel, killed for righteousness. Joseph and David are there. Job. Moses, the one who forsook fame, fortune, and pleasure for God. Jeremiah who wept. Prophets who were rejected and stoned. Peter, crucified upside down in Rome. Stephen. The five missionaries murdered by the Auca Indians. They are all calling to me, "Joe, keep on keeping on! Do your part. Complete what we through suffering have begun. Run, Joe, run!"

As I pull the baton back and clutch it tightly, I remember that in every Roman arena there is an emperor's box. An athlete coming onto the field would always look to see if the emperor were watching. And so I look. He is there. I fix my eyes on Him. It is Jesus, the author and finisher of my faith. The One who, for the joy set before Him, endured the cross (Heb. 12:2).

As I look, it is as though Jesus stands and lifts His nail-scarred hand. It's the "OK" sign. Jesus says, "Run, Joe. I have a plan and purpose. I need you. Run."

As I step onto the track, my mind focuses on all those who have gone before me. I think of David Livingstone, the pioneer missionary to Africa, who walked over 29,000 miles. His wife died early in their ministry and he faced stiff opposition from his Scottish brethren. He ministered half blind. His kind of perseverance spurs me on. As I run, I remember the words in his diary:

Send me anywhere, only go with me. Lay any burden on me, only sustain me. Sever me from any tie but the tie that binds me to Your service and to Your heart.

As we run our course, we run to the penetrating words of Isaac Watts:

> Am I a soldier of the cross,
> A follower of the Lamb?
> And shall I fear to own His cause,
> Or blush to speak His name?
>
> Must I be carried to the skies
> On flowery beds of ease,
> While others fought to win the prize,
> And sailed through bloody seas?
>
> Are there no foes for me to face?
> Must I not stem the flood?
> Is this vile world a friend to grace,
> To help me on to God?
>
> Sure I must fight, if I would reign;
> Increase my courage, Lord.
> I'll bear the toil, endure the pain,
> Supported by Thy Word.

More from Joseph Stowell

Tongue in Check
Trying to control your tongue can be frustrating—especially if you're accustomed to living by the motto, "Speak first—think later." In this book you'll learn how to develop patterns of speech that will heal, help, warm, and encourage others.

Kingdom Conflict
This book is an exposé of Satan's strategies against your commitment to Christ and His kingdom. Satan's network of evil is set to capitalize on your desires for self-fulfillment, personal glory, accumulation, and instant gratification. Learn how you can experience personal triumph in this supernatural struggle.

Dear Reader:

We would like to know your opinion of the book you've just read. Your ideas will help us as we strive to continue offering books that will satisfy your needs and interests.

Send your responses to:

Victor Books
1825 College Avenue
Wheaton, IL 60187

What most influenced your decision to purchase **THROUGH THE FIRE?**

☐ Front cover ☐ Price
☐ Title ☐ Length
☐ Author ☐ Subject
☐ Back cover material ☐ Other: _____

What did you like about this book?

☐ Helped me understand myself better ☐ Good reference tool
☐ Helped me understand others better ☐ It was easy to teach
☐ Helped me understand the Bible ☐ Author
☐ Helped me understand God

How was this book used?

☐ For my personal reading ☐ As a reference tool
☐ Studied it in a group situation ☐ Added to a church
☐ Used it to teach a group or school library

If you used this book to teach a group, did you also use the accompanying leader's guide?

☐ YES ☐ NO

Please indicate your level of interest in reading other Victor books like this one.

☐ Very interested ☐ Not very interested
☐ Somewhat interested ☐ Not at all interested

Would you recommend this book to a friend?

☐ YES ☐ NO

Please indicate your age.

☐ Under 18 ☐ 25—34 ☐ 45—54
☐ 18—24 ☐ 35—44 ☐ 55 or over

Would you like to receive more information about Victor books? If so, please fill in your name and address below:

NAME: _____

ADDRESS: _____

_____

Do you have additional comments or suggestions regarding Victor books?